APOLLO LEADERSHIP LESSONS

Powerful Business Insights for Executives

APOLLO LEADERSHIP LESSONS

Powerful Business Insights for Executives

DICK RICHARDSON

Apollo Leadership Lessons:
Powerful Insights for Business Executives

By Dick Richardson

1. BUS071000 2. BUS087000 3. BUS041000

Paperback ISBN: 978-1-949642-12-4
Hardcover ISBN: 978-1-949642-13-1
Ebook ISBN: 978-1-949642-14-8

Cover design by Lewis Agrell

Printed in the United States of America

Authority Publishing
11230 Gold Express Dr. #310-413
Gold River, CA 95670
www.AuthorityPublishing.com

Dedication

To my wife Margaret "Mimi" Richardson
who has encouraged me in every life endeavor
including this book.

TABLE OF CONTENTS

FOREWORD

I still have vivid memories of NASA's Apollo program. Destination: the Moon. President Kennedy's inspiring and audacious goal of "putting a man on the moon and returning him safely to earth" before the end of the 1960s. Overcoming the tragedy of a spacecraft fire and loss of crew. The gigantic Saturn V rocket. Astronauts in their white spacesuits headed to the launch pad. The rocket rising on a tongue of flame. Tense excitement waiting for the first landing on the moon and hearing the words "That's one small step for man; one giant leap for mankind." The gut-wrenching anticipation of returning a crippled Apollo 13 spacecraft to earth and the rallying cry of "Failure is not an option." Even though these stories are more than fifty years old, they still resonate with me today. They instilled in me a deep passion for spaceflight that continues to this day.

However, this book is not about flying in space. It is about the key people that made the Apollo program successful and the leadership insights we can gain from their stories. Dick Richardson is a masterful storyteller and highly skilled at leadership development. The combination of these traits has allowed him to use the fascinating stories of some of the prominent Apollo leaders—from astronauts to flight directors, rocket scientists to managers, presidents to administrators—and weave their significant leadership lessons into easy to understand and practical applications for today. I have been fortunate to have known and worked with many of these people and Dick is right on the mark with his analysis and leadership discussions.

I first met Dick Richardson when I attended one of his Apollo Leadership events at the Kennedy Space Center. Impressed with his ability to engage with everyone in the class and hold their attention, I listened carefully to his insights on leadership. They were simple, yet made me think carefully about how I would react in those situations and about what leadership characteristics I had that could be improved. Later on, I met Dick again at his leadership event at Gettysburg and we began a friendship that has developed over the years. C. S. Lewis said, "Friendship is the instrument by which God reveals to us the beauty of others." Dick has taught me the beauty of leaders learning from other leaders.

I have also learned that we all have stories that we have lived, and there are lessons to be learned from them. My experiences encompass flying navy fighter jets, going to space aboard the Space Shuttle, being influenced by great leaders, managing a large, diverse organization of astronauts, pilots, and engineers, and raising a large family. In all of these there are lessons that I learned and that others can learn from. Dick embodies that in himself and brings his experience in leadership development forward in telling why Apollo became successful through a relatively few key people. Those people took the United States from a lofty goal to the accomplishment of the moon landing mission that many thought was impossible. Dick Richardson is able to draw insights into how they helped lead NASA to begin the exploration of space, and how you might apply them to your situation.

Read the book. You may be spurred on to lead others to do things that are hard to do or even imagine. Whether in space or on earth, these are exciting and changing times, and you are a part of them. Dick Richardson is making a difference in helping leaders and his insights may make the journey easier and better.

David Leestma
Astronaut and former director, Flight Crew Operations Directorate Manager of NASA's Johnson Space Center Advanced Planning Office, with three completed space flights totaling over 500 hours in space.

INTRODUCTION

You've probably seen the photo of the iconic first footprint on the moon, which represents the culmination of the Apollo program. It was the fulfillment of a martyred president's vision and the first time a human being left a mark on a celestial body.

That footprint is a symbol of our desire to live, to learn, and to explore.

And it's still there...

Thanks to the lack of wind, rain, or erosion on the moon, that footprint remains, exactly as it was left by Neil Armstrong, a monument to human innovation, dedication, and leadership.

I selected that image as a metaphor for the leadership insights we can gain from NASA's Apollo Program. The legacy of the leaders who made that footprint possible is what this book is about. The impact they made continues to ripple through NASA and the world. And the lessons and takeaways we can all learn from and apply to our own lives and work environments.

Although the astronauts are the stars of the space program, it's the thousands of leaders, executives, managers, and engineers who actually made that footprint possible that we can learn from. Through their smart management decisions, the Apollo program successfully brought Americans to the moon.

This book is about those leaders, their decisions, the impact they had, and the legacy they left behind. There are many notable leaders who contributed greatly to the space program. I have selected just a few for this book.

Leaders like Wernher von Braun, who defected from Nazi Germany, bringing with him his team of skilled rocket scientists to work on the US space program. In chapter one, you'll learn how von Braun's ability to adapt as leader laid the foundation for America's rocket program. His pivotal decision to get behind the US and apply his expertise at NASA led to major breakthroughs.

And then, in chapter two, you'll hear how President Kennedy's speech at Rice University charted a course for the US space program, by presenting a vision of what could be at a time when the country was wondering if it had fallen too far behind the Russians. His message, and the way he conveyed it, is a model for communication that scholars have studied and that leaders should, too.

Chapter three profiles NASA administrator James Webb, who expertly pulled together an executive team and then built an organization around it using an innovative organizational design. The Triad, which was the three-person decision-making mechanism, consisted of Webb, Hugh Dryden, and Robert Seamans, succeeded because decisions were made by leveraging the unique expertise of each individual.

The concept of Mission Control, or the centralization of a place to monitor the performance and progress of spacecraft, was the brainchild of Christopher Columbus Kraft, Jr., or "Flight," as he would later be called. Flight was a moniker that identified and recognized what he was responsible for during manned space missions. Kraft is the subject of chapter four.

We come back to study Wernher von Braun again in chapter five, because he illustrates the value of having deep expertise in one functional area while striving to have breadth across all the areas in which executives have to lead. T-shaped leadership, as it's now called, first gained prominence in the Information Technology field. You can benefit from it too.

Chapter six draws upon the book *Hidden Figures* by Margot Shetterly and the difficulty of creating an inclusive workplace. We see how understanding social and cultural capital can allow leaders to help themselves or other people with different backgrounds to "fit in" and to support talented people to get ahead.

Becoming a leader that employees don't want to ever leave is the focus of chapter seven. It's about reciprocity. Flight Director Glynn Lunney is a prime example of a leader who helped those on his team achieve more because of his guidance and encouragement. He showed them respect and appreciation and they gave him their very best work and loyalty.

Following many years of progress toward the goal of putting a man on the moon, NASA was destined for a set-back. That occurred with Apollo 1. Fortunately, NASA had flight director Gene Kranz, who redirected everyone's attention back to the task at-hand while sorting through what had gone wrong so that it wouldn't ever happen again.

Chapter nine looks at the Apollo program after it recovered from the Apollo 1 fire and the important role George Low played in getting things back on track. The chance of another accident was high, so he had to help his team effectively balance the risk of a problem with the potential for a huge reward—the first successful moon mission.

What do you do when an unforeseen disaster occurs? How do you effectively manage a life-or-death situation? That was the scene that Apollo leaders had to contend with during the Apollo 13 crisis. For seven days, employees at every level of the organization problem-solved, using responsive innovation to address new issues that cropped up regularly as NASA worked to safely get three colleagues back home from space.

As interest in space flight continued to rise, demand for artifacts associated with space also grew, creating a new market for "flown objects." Helping to navigate new ethical waters was the domain of Deke Slayton, chief of the Astronaut Office. He had to deal with new challenges to the founding principles of NASA. Chapter eleven's focus is on ethics within the space program.

Following several successful missions that made it possible for Americans to land on the moon and safely return, NASA's next challenge was its encore. What could it do to top the achievement of its years-long goal? Answering the question, "Where do we go from here?" is a natural query that leaders have to be ready to face.

The Apollo story is rich. I hope you benefit personally and professionally from the insights offered in this book *Apollo Leadership Lessons*.

CHAPTER 1

WERNHER VON BRAUN —
ADAPTIVE LEADERSHIP IN ACTION

"Leading major organizational change often
involves radically reconfiguring a complex
network of people, tasks, and institutions that
have achieved a kind of modus vivendi, no
matter how dysfunctional it appears to you."

—Ronald Heifetz and Marty Linsky,
Harvard Business Review

Aerospace engineer Wernher von Braun was the epit-
ome of an adaptive leader. His career and dreams of
space flight were repeatedly thwarted by war, politics,

cultural rejection, organizational barriers, and, of course, technical failures. With each disruption, von Braun found a way and changed course as opportunities presented themselves. He never stopped imagining what the future could hold and strategizing different approaches to get there. While other leaders were concerned with the coming weeks or months, von Braun was always looking months or years ahead, formulating potential actions he could take to stay on course to realize his dreams of space flight.

While in Germany working under Hitler's rule, von Braun recognized that Germany would soon lose World War II. He needed a plan. He wanted a way for his team to surrender to the Americans. He imagined several possible scenarios and planned for each, hoping to be brought to the US to continue working on his rocketry program. Once in the US, he continued to adapt and reposition himself. He rebranded himself from enemy to skilled aerospace engineer to friendly scientist. And in doing so, he made possible stunning accomplishments in space exploration.

The Apollo space program succeeded because of adaptive leaders who could solve new, unique and, thus, "adaptive problems." Usually we face problems that are similar to ones we've seen before. Scholars call these technical problems. Unlike technical problems, which have occurred before and provide a reference point for possible solutions, adaptive problems have not been seen before; there is no history to refer back to, only future possibilities. The space program was full of adaptive problems and not all leaders had the capacity to look ahead and conceive new approaches.

Fortunately, von Braun did.

Career as Business

Von Braun's lifelong obsession with space began at age thirteen, when his mother gave him a telescope for his birthday. That curiosity about the moon and stars gave way to a life mission to travel into space, or to make such travel possible for others. Space travel and rocketry soon became his sole focus academically, where he did well enough in math and science to be advanced to graduate from high school a year early.

The Rest of the Story

Young Wernher started his interest in astronomy with his telescope. But the real turning point in his life occurred a year later when he read the book *Die Rakete zu den Planetenräumen* ("The Rocket into Interplanetary Space") by Hermann Oberth, a rocket[1] pioneer. As an adult, von Braun asked his hero, Oberth, to come and work with him at Peenemünde in 1941. Oberth helped von Braun for two years then moved on to other work for the German Army. After the war, Oberth settled in Italy working on rockets for the Italian Navy. When von Braun and his team joined the United States Army in Huntsville, Alabama, he again sought out his teacher Oberth. They worked together until 1958 when Oberth moved back to Germany. He came to the US as von Braun's guest to witness the Saturn V rocket launch of Apollo 11 to the moon.

Long before von Braun was given responsibility for the US rocket program, he studied at the University of Berlin. While there he was recruited by the Wehrmacht (German Army) as an intern. His technical ability was obvious. He quickly rose through the ranks. He was also a skilled technical manager, able to lead teams of experts to find solutions to problems that regularly vexed others. He joined the German Army rocket team, moved to Peenemünde, and within a few short years was responsible for hundreds of engineers, scientists, and other staff. While apolitical, von Braun did join the SS in order to progress working in the field; he was told that, essentially, he had no choice.

By 1944, it became clear to von Braun that Germany would lose the war. Unfortunately, he voiced those concerns one night while under the influence and was reported to the Gestapo[2] by a spy for being a "defeatist." He was arrested and then jailed for two weeks. He might have been left there if not for his critical role in the development of the V-2 rocket. His release was granted with the understanding that the rocket must succeed.

German military and civilian leaders began assessing their options, given that seemingly inevitable conclusion to the conflict. They perceived their choices to be: continue fighting for their homes and the Fatherland, take off their uniforms and blend in with the thousands of refugees escaping through Europe, travel through Switzerland or the Vatican as a path to South America, or surrender.

Von Braun weighed those choices. But he saw another way out that no one else had seemed to consider. He wanted more than to merely survive in a new country, he wanted to be able to continue his work on rocketry alongside his colleagues from Peenemünde.

He carefully plotted his next move, considering all the various scenarios and potential ramifications. Given the various forces nearing his team's location, he believed his choices for takeover were Russia, whose army was quickly closing in; France; England; or the US. For von Braun, the choice was easy—he wanted to work in the US.

Von Braun approached this like a business problem. This was similar to an acquisition or merger. What steps could he take to make his team at Peenemünde an attractive acquisition target? He wanted the US to "acquire" his business. To be sure the US would be interested, von Braun knew he needed to have something of value to offer the US military. Fortunately, he did. He had the V-2, the world's first ballistic missile.

Photograph of Wernher von Braun with V2 Rocket model
taken at Marshall Space Flight Center

What he really had was the intellectual property to
build a missile. He needed to ensure that he had continued possession of the proprietary details of the V-2. He
couldn't let them be destroyed by the Germans or stolen
by other military forces. So, he started hiding things.

He secreted away plans, schematics, wiring diagrams, and test results in farmers' barns and other buildings. He hid rocket parts in an abandoned iron mine in the Harz Mountains and blew up the entrance. The real place where intellectual property exists is in people's minds. He broached the subject of surrendering to his team. Once they agreed, he collaborated with an SS general to move his team to Bavaria and had them disperse, ostensibly to avoid being killed as a group by an air raid. Their true goal, he told them, was to find and surrender themselves to American troops.

Unbeknownst to von Braun at the time, the US was already looking for him. Project Paperclip's[3] secret mission was to capture key German technologies and scientists, including von Braun and many members of his team. So, when von Braun's brother Magnus stole a bicycle and rode toward American soldiers to arrange for his brother's surrender, the reconnaissance patrol that met him was more than happy to take him in.

But the welcome was not what von Braun had imagined. American forces imprisoned him and his men and moved them around Europe during the summer of 1945. But understanding his interest in working with the US, the US Army offered von Braun and 126 members of his team a six-month contract to make rockets for the army in Fort Bliss, Texas. This was a controversial move at the time, since President Truman had ordered that anyone who was found to have been a member of the Nazi party would be ineligible to work for the US; von Braun and many on his team had served as Nazi officers. Fortunately for von Braun, the US was so intent on winning the Cold War that participation in the Nazi party was scrubbed[4] from his records as well as his colleagues' official records.

Leadership Insight

Wernher von Braun illustrates the characteristics of an adaptive leader, but there are questions about his ethics. Slave labor was used later in the war in the manufacturing of V-2 rockets at Mittelwork. The workers lived in deplorable conditions and over 20,000 died of exhaustion and malnutrition. The production facilities did not report to von Braun, but we know he visited the site.

Leaders often face ethical dilemmas. For von Braun, it was the use of slave labor to build his dream rockets. For the US government, it was whether to accept and employ von Braun or hold him accountable for his association with the Nazi crimes. In these cases, it's often the balance between the mission and objectives versus ethics and values.

Business leaders often face ethical dilemmas. Take the automotive industry for example. John DeLorean turned to smuggling cocaine to finance the manufacturing of his dream car. In his quest to make Volkswagen the number one carmaker in the world, CEO Martin Winterkorn led a global effort to falsify emission tests. Volkswagen has paid billions in fines in return for his ethical decision. Nissan/

Renault Chairman Carlos Ghosn resigned after disclosure of tax irregularities.

As leaders, we can face a slippery slope in pursuit of success.

When the Korean War broke out in 1950, von Braun and his team moved to the Redstone Arsenal in Huntsville, Alabama. He was promoted to director of the operations division. As von Braun rose in the ranks of the US space program, he was also having success in adapting to America.

He saw that a path to repositioning or rebranding himself, not as the German enemy, but as a harmless scientist, could begin with the media. He began submitting articles on the peaceful exploration of space in the hopes of changing his image. *The Huntsville Times* published one, followed by another in the national *Collier's* magazine which, at the time, had four million subscribers. The article was so well received that he published four more between 1952 and 1954.

Despite rising interest in his articles on space flight, von Braun once again recognized the emergence of a new opportunity—in television. By 1952, there were already fifteen million TVs in American homes[5] and von Braun saw it as a tool to further his message supporting peaceful space exploration. He approached Walt Disney about collaborating on television specials and on a new exhibit at Disneyland to be called

"Tomorrowland." I remember sitting cross-legged in front of our black-and-white TV in the late fifties watching the *Wonderful World of Disney*. On my television set were "Uncle Walt" Disney, Mickey Mouse, and "Uncle Wernher" who introduced the show on space travel.

With the 1957 Russian launch of the satellite Sputnik, pressure was on the US to catch up in the "space race." Von Braun offered to work on getting a US satellite into orbit, but the Vanguard research rocket was selected instead. Broadcast live on TV, it blew up on the launchpad. Von Braun was waiting for his opportunity. The Vanguard failure was it. He said, "We have the hardware on the shelf. We can put up a satellite in sixty days." America needed a savior and Wernher came through. He succeeded, launching Explorer 1. Some of his other accomplishments included designing the Vertical Assembly Building (VAB), multiple launch sites, the Crawler transporter, and many others, because he was constantly imagining what would make space exploration possible.

When NASA was formed in 1958, von Braun was offered a role, but he didn't want just any job, he wanted to be responsible for developing a huge rocket capable of landing on the moon. He was promoted to deputy associate administrator for planning at NASA headquarters in Washington, DC.

The Importance of Environmental Scans

Von Braun's greatest strength was his intellect and strategic mind. He was forever imagining different futures for himself, his team, and his country, finding new potential paths to achieve his vision of space exploration. By thinking through the myriad potential next steps in his career, he was always prepared to adapt and pivot as needed.

He was unusual in that regard.

We humans get tunnel vision easily. We tend to focus almost exclusively on our area of expertise—the lane that we're swimming in, as it were—to ensure we're up-to-date and well-informed about industry happenings. Engineers focus on shifts occurring in the engineering field, marketers focus on changes in marketing that are underway, and financial pros are immersed in financial industry fluctuations.

We're seldom surprised by changes in our area of expertise, because that's what we're immersed in daily. We are, however, surprised by changes that have taken place outside our domains of expertise. Engineers are caught off-guard by social changes. Politicians are surprised by technology advances. Physicians are unaware of marketing opportunities or shifts. We lose sight of the broader picture.

Adaptive leaders, like von Braun, avoid the trap of being hyper-focused on one area and excluding others by constantly scanning their environment. They routinely look outside their normal spheres of interest to stay current on larger issues. The result is a level of flexibility and adaptability to change that can be a source of competitive advantage.

An environmental scan is a macro assessment of the factors that could affect an organization's strategy. Environmental scans can be very detailed and complex, or more ad hoc. The goal of such scans is to provide leaders with situational awareness—to be more aware of the forces that could impact their organization positively or negatively.

This improved level of awareness then makes leaders adept at identifying threats or opportunities and more effective at developing and executing new strategies. They are better able to take advantage of opportunities that are identified. Conversely, they can also anticipate and mitigate negative forces that arise. They are prepared.

Leaders should routinely examine multiple environmental factors to broaden their perspectives. These factors include, but are not limited to:

- **Politics and government.** This includes regulatory agencies and legislation such as Brexit, net neutrality, and two-for-one regulation repeal.

- **Social and demographic changes.** These include events such as the evolving definition of gender, LGBTQI issues, immigration, generational conflicts, and dislocation.

- **Legal.** Recent legal issues include our increasingly litigious society, automated legal systems, and changing Chinese treatment of intellectual property, for example.

- **Geophysical.** Climate change and conflict are two types of geophysical events that drive economic and population shifts.

- **Technological.** Monitoring constant changes in technology is smart, where we're currently seeing advances in artificial intelligence that affect future employment and the rise in ransomware, for example.

- **Economic.** Economic events like the rising price of oil, housing bubbles, and currency fluctuations can also impact future opportunities.

- **Competitors and suppliers.** As barriers to entry and exit rise and fall, new competitors emerge. We've seen this as Amazon moves into brick-and-mortar through its recent acquisition of Whole Foods. New suppliers can be formed, changing the marketplace dynamic.

- **Customers.** Shifting consumer demographics, rising preference for online transactions, and the impact of social media on shopping habits are all issues impacting customers.

Constantly monitoring and studying what is happening in all eight of these areas provides leaders with a broader, richer understanding of their environment—past, present, and future. But environmental scanning, as this monitoring is called, is not just about identifying trends. Trends are individual pieces of information. Environmental scanning involves analyzing and interpreting what all the trends together mean, now and in the future, and how they can affect you.

The bigger, deeper, and longer the evaluation is, the more thorough the scan and the better your ability to map out all the potential outcomes. By bigger I mean how broad or wide an analysis you're conducting; studying some or all of the above factors. By deeper I mean how earnestly you're questioning your assumptions. And longer meaning temporal—looking longer into the future to map out potential outcomes.

Your goal isn't to identify the one most likely path to success, but rather the myriad different possible paths. Then, how best to respond depending on the specific path taken. And as each environmental change forces a course correction toward your goal, new potential paths also emerge. The best leaders are constantly adjusting their paths to account for new market shifts. That's how von Braun thought—he scanned his environment to try and picture all the possible outcomes, and then envisioned possible pathways to his desired result, taking action according to changes in his environment. The key was being hyper aware of all the changes occurring around him.

Von Braun, for example, stayed current on events occurring in the military, political, economic, legal, and social environment in 1944, rather than focusing intently on the technical projects assigned to him, as many of his colleagues and other technical leaders did. For that reason, he was better informed and could envision potential future options those around him could never have imagined.

Leadership Insight

Recent years have been marked by increased awareness and controversy of the many challenges leaders face in diversity and inclusion. A good part of von Braun's success can be attributed to his ability to understand the world through other people's eyes. He reached out to members of the media, politicians, business leaders, economists, and others outside his normal scientific and cultural community. He understood the need for diversity of perspectives. He also went the next step—the deliberate act of welcoming those perspectives to help him and his team to anticipate change and adapt.

One way von Braun ensured diversity of thought was by moving many of his best people out of his organization. For example, of the 126 scientists who came with him after the war, Kurt Debus became the Center Director at NASA Kennedy Space Center, Ernst Eckert moved to the US Air Force, Krafft Ehricke became an executive at Bell Aerospace, etc. In turn, von Braun sought out new and heterogeneous talent for his organization.

Creating Alternate Futures

This ability to adapt, to zig and then zag, based on unexpected environmental shifts is a core skill of adaptive leaders. These are the individuals who are able to steer an organization through major transformation, through challenges that it has never faced before.

This "wrenching organizational transformation," as Ronald Heifetz and Marty Linsky refer to it in their *Harvard Business Review* piece titled, "A Survival Guide for Leaders"[6] is very different from the everyday "technical change" that leaders routinely face. Technical change is caused by technical problems that the organization has faced before, where there is a known solution. Adaptive change, in contrast, has never been seen before and has no immediately identifiable solution. In fact, the solution is that the organization and those within it need to change their behavior. A leader is needed to guide people through that change.

Heifetz and Linsky call adaptive leadership "an improvisational art," because it's impossible to strategize and plan too far in the future, if at all, during radical organizational change. Adaptive leaders must simultaneously pay attention to the day-to-day details of what's happening within their organizations as well as the 35,000-foot view, where they get a broader perspective on what's happening and why. "Sustaining good leadership, then, requires first and foremost the capacity to see what is happening to you and your initiative as it is happening and to understand how today's turns in the road will affect tomorrow's plans," explain Heifetz and Linsky.

Von Braun was capable of adapting because he was constantly looking at his situation and his ecosystem from multiple perspectives. Most leaders get so caught up in their own world, and their own problems, that they fail to take a broader view of their situation. In contrast, von Braun regularly looked outside of his normal spheres of interest. In doing so, he recognized one of many paths he and his team could take. As his environment shifted, his strategies shifted, which sometimes required unconventional action by his team.

He considered differing perspectives and "what-ifs" more than other leaders. This was never more evident than in 1944, when he drew very different conclusions than the German leaders about the ongoing war. Considering many different and even conflicting perspectives, von Braun saw an end in the near future where Germany would not be victorious. German leaders, on the other hand, who were hyper-focused on the military and political battlefield could only see certain victory. Von Braun was right, they were wrong.

Adaptive leaders gather information in order to understand their environment and are constantly analyzing it in order to assess what to do about it, keeping their ultimate goal in the forefront of their minds. Von Braun's ultimate goal was making spaceflight possible. Everything he did during the tumult of World War II enabled him to extricate himself and hundreds of members of his team from Nazi Germany to emigrate to the US and become essential participants in the US space program. In addition to effectively reacting to the change around him, von Braun also initiated his own personal metamorphosis, transforming himself from the enemy to a valued and trusted member of NASA and celebrity status as a popular writer and minor TV personality.

While adaptive leadership occurs during times of great change, it's also what makes great progress possible. Adaptive leadership leverages past knowledge and experience and mobilizes teams to foster progress beyond what was previously thought possible. Adaptive leaders make impossible things possible. That's exactly what NASA needed at the time.

Leadership Experience

To help you apply what you've learned about adaptive leadership and Wernher von Braun's work within NASA, consider these questions:

- What is your guiding vision? Think long term strategically and mid-term operationally.

- How can you gain different perspectives of your organization's environment?

- How can you do more contingency planning—imagining alternate paths to achieving your ends?

- What allies will you need to be successful?

- What are you willing to sacrifice and not sacrifice to achieve your goals?

CHAPTER 2

JOHN F. KENNEDY — NURTURING A VISION

"Keep your eyes on the stars and your
feet on the ground."

—Franklin D. Roosevelt

I learned a simple definition of leadership from General John Wattendorf, Department Head, Behavioral Sciences and Leadership at West Point Military Academy. *"Leadership is influencing others to do what they would not do if left to their own accord."*

Leaders have many ways of influencing others, but a primary method is through one-to-many communication—presentations, broadcasts, and, of course, speeches. Some have estimated that more than thirty million presentations are given each day. Most presentations are meant to influence someone. So, what makes a speech or presentation by a leader effective in influencing others?

Consider the most memorable speeches meant to persuade people: Martin Luther King Jr.'s 1963 "I have a dream…" speech, Lincoln's Gettysburg Address, Susan B Anthony's "Webster, Worcester, and Bouvier…" speech on women's right to vote, and John F. Kennedy's "We choose to go to the moon" speech at Rice University.

What made these speeches so persuasive was not necessarily their oration, but their vision and appeal to the heart as well as the mind. These leaders understood the importance of painting a picture of possibility as a first step toward making their vision a reality. Once visualized, their challenge was bringing that goal to fruition.

Focusing on the Future

One could use the line from Dickens' A *Tale of Two Cities* to describe the country's mood when John F. Kennedy took office in January 1961: "It was the best of times and the worst of times."

The economy was good and the Korean War was over, but domestically, the social justice causes of civil rights and women's rights were growing. Americans were discouraged that the US had been repeatedly bested in the race into space by the Soviet Union. They questioned the leadership—or even viability—of the country's space program. Yet the country was also hopeful that President Kennedy was the man to turn the situation around.

Why go to the moon? Understanding his reality and responsibility as the country's leader, Kennedy took to the podium at Rice University's football stadium and delivered perhaps the most famous of all speeches about space exploration to a crowd of around 40,000 students, faculty, congressmen, and government officials. He challenged Americans to move past the country's failure to get a man into space first and to look ahead to the future—a future that could include putting an American on the moon. It would take hardship and hard work, and a massive budget, but if everyone was committed, we could get there in ten years, he promised.

But the truth was, Kennedy had just endured a harrowing first 100 days in office. Shortly after becoming president, he experienced a series of challenges that put him and the entire country on the defensive and, to some degree, damaged his credibility.

The first was the Soviet Union's successful launch of cosmonaut Yuri Gagarin into space aboard the Vostok 1 on April 12, 1961. The fact that the Soviets had put a man into a low-Earth orbit first was felt as a loss for the US, which was now perceived as trailing the Soviet's capabilities.

Then, only five days later, was the disastrous Bay of Pigs invasion that wasn't. The clandestine invasion of Cuba was an attempt to overthrow Fidel Castro. It failed. The Central Intelligence Agency landed 1500 Cubans along with CIA agents on Cuba's southernmost spot—The Bay of Pigs. Castro had caught wind of the pending attack and was ready. Nearly 1,000 of the brigade were captured and 114 killed during the three-day offensive.

It was another loss attributed to the new president.

Kennedy and the country needed a win. Although Kennedy had been mulling over whether to shutter the US manned space program[7] and give up on space flight altogether due to the cost, the Soviet's surprising success and the nation's reaction got his attention. He knew that the US couldn't compete head-to-head with the USSR. They were ahead in every way. Kennedy began looking for other options—a way to change the playing field, as it were.

"Where can we beat these guys?"

On April 20 Kennedy asked Vice President Lyndon Johnson to consult with NASA experts about where the US could succeed against the Soviets. Said space policy expert John Logsdon[8], author of *John F. Kennedy and the Race to the Moon*, Johnson's marching orders were to find "a space program which promises dramatic results in which we could win." NASA administrator James Webb and leading rocket scientist Wernher von Braun both reported that the USA could beat the USSR to the moon. However, it could take ten years. Actually, von Braun said, the US had "a sporting chance."

At times, a winning vision is enough. The moon became Kennedy's new rallying cry.

But it wasn't so much because of a personal interest in space exploration as it was a means to regaining the upper hand politically; Kennedy had little interest in the study of space. As *The Atlantic* reports it, historian

Sept 12, 1962, President John F. Kennedy delivers his famous "Why go to the moon" speech at Rice Stadium in Houston, Texas. NASA Photo s67-19620

Dwayne Day, Phd[9] explained, "Kennedy was interested in space as a symbol of political power, but it was only after the Soviet Union increased the political stakes that Kennedy approved the lunar landing program."

He first addressed the country's defeat in space and its future plans during a May 25 speech to the Joint Session of Congress. It would take ten years, $531 million in 1961 and "$7 to $9 billion additional over the next five years," but we will put a man on the moon, he promised, stating:

> "...we have examined where we are strong and where we are not, where we may succeed and where we may not. Now it is time to take longer strides-time for a great new American enterprise-time for this nation to take a clearly leading role in space achievement, which in many ways may hold the key to our future on earth."

That speech to Congress was Kennedy's opening salvo. It was the first time he revealed his intentions and was a chance for him to test the waters regarding his lofty goal. It hit home. Many leaders mistakenly set a goal and then leave it. Kennedy knew that a vision had to be nurtured and reinforced repeatedly. So, he honed his message for more of a citizen audience—the folks who would be in attendance at Rice University in Houston, Texas, that fall.

Leadership Insight

As we saw in chapter one, all leaders lead within an environment. Just as Wernher von Braun scanned his environment and adjusted, JFK did the same. The competition from the Soviet Union and setbacks in other areas, both foreign and domestic, caused Kennedy to pivot.

Kennedy had campaigned on civil rights, education, and economic progress. Those causes were close to his heart. As he shifted the focus to the space program, he used it as a means to his ends in those other areas. NASA became a public sector leader in eliminating segregation. NASA administrator James Webb insisted that "every dollar spent should return two." The second dollar was often grants to universities funneled through NASA contractors. The billions spent on space boosted the economy. Leaders often find ways to achieve multiple ends from a single project.

Kennedy at Rice

Kennedy's "We go to the moon" speech, as it soon became known, marked a turning point for the US in terms of its space program. No more would America stand to be second-best, Kennedy seemed to say to the crowd of space enthusiasts, as nearly all Americans were at that time.

While this speech will long be remembered for the success that it was, it followed a fairly common structure for enrollment speeches—speeches where the orator has an agenda, or is trying to convince the audience to get on board with his idea. Enrollment speeches are meant to persuade.

One approach, which he used, is to provide some history for context, to address the challenge at-hand, and paint a picture of the possible future: past, present, future. Another is to weave logos, pathos, and ethos— logic, emotion, and credibility—throughout, to drive key points home. Kennedy did both in his speech at Rice.

The Past

Kennedy started by talking about the past and what led the US to its current situation. He described in detail the breakneck pace at which technology was evolving, likening 50,000 years of human history to fifty years:

> "…condense,[10] if you will, the 50,000 years of man's recorded history in a time span of but a half-century."

Continuing with this analogy, he said: "Then about ten years ago, under this standard, man emerged from his caves to construct other kinds of shelter. Only five years ago man learned to write and use a cart with wheels." And at this pace, man will have "literally reached the stars before midnight tonight."

Kennedy wanted to propose that reaching the moon was almost within our grasp, should we choose to travel there; that our past has now presented us with this opportunity.

The Present

His speech then shifted to the present, hinting at the fact that no matter what we do, Russia would continue with its space program: "the exploration of space will go ahead, whether we join in it or not." But he also began to sow seeds of fear—what if the Russians got there first? America would surely be at a disadvantage, which could be dangerous.

He referenced the country's "hopes for peace and security" and "our obligations to ourselves as well as others," suggesting that we owed it to ourselves as Americans, and to our allies, to invest in space exploration. The US must "become the world's leading space-faring nation" in order to increase our own safety and security.

Traveling to the moon became a necessity to preserve our way of life, Kennedy inferred. And few people back then dared disagree with him.

The Future

In order to achieve this objective of landing on the moon inside of ten years, Kennedy then described what the country had already done to prepare for this future endeavor. He talked about the investments that had already been made in facilities, technology, Saturn rockets, and satellites, and the benefit to the American people of investing their hard-earned tax dollars in the mission—namely, a growing availability of high-paying jobs for skilled scientists. By committing to this future mission, Americans would secure their way of life and create new opportunities for themselves.

Parallel to this presentation of history, current challenges, and future achievements, Kennedy used the framework of logos, pathos, and ethos to sway the American public—to influence them. These three themes are at the heart of effective enrollment speeches.

Logos

Logos, or logic, is one element that Kennedy used throughout his Rice speech. He described all the investments made up to that point in space exploration and crafted a logical argument for why the US needed to invest at a more aggressive rate in order to gain the upper hand against the Soviet Union.

Each section of his speech built on the last as he systematically made a case for going all-in on travel to the moon.

Pathos

Americans were already on edge after Russia demonstrated superiority in space; they were fearful. So, Kennedy leveraged that insecurity, tapping into that fear and expressing sympathy for those real feelings.

That Russia might soon control the skies created a security weakness for the US, he asserted. Allowing our enemies to beat us could have damaging repercussions, he told us. The result of this is anxiety and worry.

He also touched on positive emotions. He appealed to our pride: "But this city of Houston, this State of Texas, this country of the United States was not built by those who waited and rested and wished to look behind them. This country was conquered by those who moved forward—and so will space."

Ethos

Kennedy also demonstrated source credibility or authority—ethos—as he spoke, so that those in the audience did not question his statements. He cited Newton for reference: "Newton explored the meaning of gravity."

Then he quoted from one of our founding fathers: "William Bradford, speaking in 1630 of the founding of the Plymouth Bay Colony, said that all great and honorable actions are accompanied with great difficulties, and both must be enterprised and overcome with answerable courage."

On top of making a logical case for investing heavily in space exploration, Kennedy made Americans feel. They were afraid, then hopeful, then resolved, and then proud of the ambitious plan their president had outlined.

The Rest of the Story

Aristotle is credited with identifying the elements of influence: logos, ethos, and pathos. His treatise *Rhetoric* is regarded by scholars as "the most important single work on persuasion ever written." Many leaders today rely too heavily on logos or logic. We produce PowerPoint slides with huge amounts of information rationale and data.

The best leaders recognize that rationale is important, but only one part of influence. Trust in the speaker and an emotional connection are key to influencing others, subordinates, and even superiors.

Speech Length

Short is good. Some of the most memorable speeches have been among the shortest on record. Abraham Lincoln's Gettysburg Address was only two minutes long and he had only been invited to provide "concluding remarks;"[11] he was not the keynote of the day. That honor went to the former Secretary of State Edward Everett, who tried to say in two hours what it took Lincoln mere seconds. Lincoln's uncharacteristic brevity that day may have made his words even more memorable.

Most enrollment speeches take longer than two minutes, however. When asked about how long it took him to prepare a speech, President Woodrow Wilson stated:[12]

"It depends. If I am to speak ten minutes, I need a week for preparation; if fifteen minutes, three days; if half an hour, two days; if an hour, I am ready now."

Modern day TED Talks are between ten and eighteen minutes—but never more than eighteen minutes—because that has been found to be the optimal length for holding the audience's attention and making a point. TED curator Chris Anderson[13] explained:

"It [eighteen minutes] is long enough to be serious and short enough to hold people's attention. It turns out that this length also works incredibly well online. It's the length of a coffee break."[14]

No one is exempt from this limit, which forces even the best orators to distill their thinking down in such a way that the audience can more easily apply it.

Kennedy's Rice speech was seventeen minutes and forty-eight seconds.

Communication Patterns

Every leader is at some point called on to give an enrollment speech. It may be in response to a new threat by a competing company, bad news that has dampened employee morale, or an opportunity that will require a doubling of effort and commitment. In addition to determining how best to present information about your current situation—the big themes—also think about how you'll deliver this information.

As you listen to Kennedy's speech, you will probably notice the following about his speech patterns and speaking style:

- **Simple words.** Kennedy doesn't try to impress by using multisyllabic words no one recognizes. Instead, he used words everyone in the audience is familiar with. He makes the information he's sharing accessible, understandable.

- **Short sentences.** Kennedy also makes sure not to use run-on sentences with several ideas or concepts jumbled together. He uses short, crisp sentences containing a single idea at a time.

- **Systematic.** Each sentence builds on the last, like stepping stones on a path to his key point. When Kennedy makes a statement, he then backs it up with an explanation or proof. He makes his point in a methodical way.

- **No extra fluff.** He chooses his words carefully, packing a punch in as few words as possible. There's little in the way of extraneous verbiage here, but he does choose words that generate an emotional response whenever possible, such as "pride" or "un-tried."

- **Repetition.** Many of the great speeches, including Kennedy's, use repetition for effect.

Abraham Lincoln repeated the words "can not" in the Gettysburg address: "Can not dedicate…can not consecrate…can not hallow…" and "of the people, by the people, for the people." Similarly, Kennedy used the phrase "We choose" three times in his speech, just as Martin Luther King, Jr. used the phrase "Now is the time."

Kennedy's speech at Rice has become a quintessential example of how to nurture a vision—in this case, of reaching the moon.

So, what is your vision for your organization? What needs to happen next to get you on the path to success? How will you share and nurture that vision within your company?

Leadership Insight

When I asked General Wattendorf to review this chapter, he wrote a thoughtful comment on simplicity that I believe should be noted. "I like simple definitions. However, I continue to be concerned that 'leadership' is not simple. For example, in my view, leadership is not to be equated with coercion. When persons do what a leader has influenced them to do, they will do it whether or not the leader is present. In other words, the followers internalize the desire to accomplish the tasks/goals established or communicated by the leader. Additionally, in the case of 'organizational leadership,' the influence must be consistent with the goals and values of the organization. Leaders not only influence followers to want to do what they otherwise might not do (because they didn't think of it, or because they previously did not want to do it), but also leaders do what they can to help others accomplish these assigned tasks and goals. They enhance the abilities of others by providing requisite knowledge, tools, and materials. Finally, I always emphasized the ethical dimension of what I call 'true' leadership. Leaders influence others to do what is right."

Leadership Experience

Crafting your own enrollment speeches will be easier after you study some of the great ones that have been given. Watch these videos and read these transcripts of past speeches to reinforce what you've just learned about them.

- Kennedy at Rice: https://www.youtube.com/watch?v=ouRbkBAOGEw

- Susan B. Anthony: http://www.historyplace.com/speeches/anthony.htm

- Frederick Douglass: http://www.pbs.org/wgbh/aia/part4/4h2927t.html

- Martin Luther King, Jr.: http://www.
  teachertube.com/video/i-have-a-dream-
  speech-martin-luther-king-jr-video-20916

- Steve Jobs: https://news.stanford.edu/2005/06/
  14/jobs-061505/

Then, spend some time thinking through how you
influence people. Ask yourself:

- Is my message short and clear?

- Do I use the framework of past—present—
  future?

- Do I use Ethos and Pathos as well as Logos
  to make my case?

CHAPTER 3

JAMES WEBB — INNOVATION AND ORGANIZATIONAL DESIGN

"Great things in business are never done by one person. They're done by a team of people."

—Steve Jobs in *Steve Jobs: His Own Words and Wisdom*

James Webb was an unlikely candidate to become the administrator of NASA, succeeding Keith Glennan. He was unlikely because there was nothing in his experience or education to indicate he could lead a large technical organization. He was a finance guy, not an aerospace engineer or scientist. In fact, most people around him felt he was not well-suited to a career in aerospace.

Despite being essentially forced into a position he didn't want and wasn't prepared for, Webb made it his own, transforming how decisions were made at the top within NASA and introducing policies that leveraged his strengths and reduced the impact of his weaknesses. With 20/20 hindsight we can now see that he was an excellent choice to shape the leadership of NASA. Additionally, his approach to management can serve as an effective model in many organizations.

Developing a Future Leader

Webb grew up in North Carolina, the son of two teachers. After the stock market crash of 1929, and with prospects limited in a small town, he joined the Marine Corps and was hand-picked to be part of the first aviation squad in the Corps, where he worked alongside "privileged Ivy-Leaguers."[15] Rather than feeling like the odd man out, however, Webb "discovered he could match or even outstrip the achievements of people more privileged than himself."[16]

That was a life-changing lesson that shaped how he viewed his future prospects. After the Marine Corps, he enrolled in law school, which introduced him to a new circle of friends. Many were government officials; he "turned out to be a smart political operator."[17] He then landed a job as a secretary to North Carolina Senator Edward Pou and made more political friends. He developed a reputation as being good with numbers—a strong financier. He joined a local law firm and was then recruited to work at the Sperry Corporation. At Sperry, he leveraged his knowledge of law and aviation and helped scale operations to become a successful defense contractor. Although he would never have considered himself a technologist, he became adept at getting things done inside a technology company.

When the war started, he returned to active duty in the Marine Corps, where he coordinated the use of radar control by night fighters in the Pacific. The planes had to determine how to attack enemies without hitting US troops.

After World War II, Webb returned to public service. He was promoted to director of the bureau of the budget under President Truman. He worked hard to keep military spending in check and was later promoted to Under Secretary of State.

Webb was approached by Vice President Johnson and asked to consider assuming the role of NASA administrator. Webb asked for two weeks to think about it. During that time, he did more than think—he actively assessed his own strengths and weaknesses and asked for feedback from the people around him—an informal 360-degree assessment. He wanted an objective appraisal of his ability to succeed in the NASA role.

The people who knew him best told him that the NASA job required skills he did not have. He was weak in his understanding of technology and weak in operational experience—two skills that would be critical for success leading a large highly-technical organization.

He also approached leaders in aerospace and asked them what kinds of skills were needed to do such a job well. The types of abilities they mentioned as being critical for success were also not on Webb's list of personal strengths. Most people felt that not only was Webb not the best choice for the role—he wasn't even qualified.

Given what he had gleaned about the space program and where he might fit, Webb stated that, "I would not take the job if I could honorably and properly not take it."[18] Meaning, unless forced into it, he would decline.

Webb was asked to come to Washington to meet with Johnson about the job offer. Following several meetings and the general consensus that he was not the right candidate, Webb told NASA deputy administrator Hugh Dryden to please convey the message to Johnson that he needed to decline. "I don't believe he wants to listen to me on that," he told Webb.

So, he appealed to ally and friend Frank Pace, the CEO of General Dynamics. Pace also tried to change Johnson's mind, but without success. Seventeen other candidates had already declined the opportunity. Johnson was fed up—he didn't want an eighteenth refusal.[19] Pace entered Johnson's office to relay the message that Webb didn't want the job. Webb waited in the anteroom. Pace quickly came out and Johnson yelled out his office door, "Webb, get in here!"

James Webb in a typical supporting role to the president and astronauts. Ceremony to celebrate the success of the first spacewalk. Left to right, James Webb, astronaut James McDivitt, Robert Seamans Jr., President Johnson, astronaut Edward White II. NASA Photo s65-33250

Forty-five minutes later he was the new NASA administrator.

Few people, including Webb, were thrilled with the selection. *Aviation Week & Space Technology* magazine expressed its lack of confidence in Webb's skills. "The president should have appointed a technically competent manager."

The Dunning-Kruger Effect

Webb had tried valiantly to avoid falling victim to the Dunning-Kruger effect. Dunning and Kruger are Cornell psychology professors whose research found that people are poor judges of their own skills and abilities. That is, there is a general tendency (especially by men) to overestimate one's own skills. Or, as David Dunning explained to *The Atlantic*,[20] "incompetent people do not recognize—scratch that, cannot recognize—just how incompetent they are."

Competent people also have a tendency to overestimate their capabilities. In a 2000 study of Stanford MBA students,[21] eighty-seven percent rated their academic performance as above average. Given that only fifty percent of the class could actually be above the median, a large percentage of students in the class has overestimated their GPA and, perhaps, their skills. The study found that less proficient individuals were much more likely to overestimate their own level of skill and to downplay the true talents of others. However, the Dunning-Kruger trap isn't limited to the less-skilled, only more likely to appear.

The truth is, even gifted athletes have fallen victim—Michael Jordan, for example. Jordan is certainly one of the top three or four basketball players of all time. Named "Athlete of the Century" by ESPN, he is among the very elite in terms of athletic skill. Where he stumbled, however, was in assuming that his basketball prowess would carry over into other sports.

When Jordan retired from basketball the first time, in 1993, he had his eye on playing baseball for the Chicago White Sox. He loved baseball, maybe even more than basketball, and hoped to begin a new career.

So, he signed with the White Sox as a free agent in 1994 and was assigned to the AA Birmingham Barons of the Southern League, a minor league team, to give him some experience. He expected that he would soon be moved up to the majors.

In his first season, Jordan was a marginal hitter at best, batting .202 with 51 RBIs, 30 stolen bases, and 114 strikeouts in 127 games, according to the North Carolina Tar Heels website.[22] Certainly not the standout that he may have been hoping to be. That fall he played for the Scottsdale Scorpions, batting .252 in thirty-five games during the fall league season—slightly better than his debut season but still a subpar performance.

The following spring, he walked out of training camp. Reported Brian Willett[23] on Jordan's foray into baseball: "After his relatively unsuccessful season playing baseball, Jordan decided to return to the NBA. Jordan issued a press release on March 18, 1995, that stated simply, 'I'm back,' and returned to the Chicago Bulls the next day."

Although Jordan had succumbed to the Dunning-Kruger trap, Webb tried hard not to. He maintained an objective view of himself and what he had to offer, which is why he was fairly certain from the outset that he was not the best pick to be NASA administrator. And yet, when his vice president asked him to take the job, he was unable to turn it down.

Leadership Insight

Interestingly, women are less prone to overestimating their skills and abilities than men. That is, women are more likely to discount their talents and experience than men. Books such as *The Confidence Code* by Katty Kay and Claire Shipman, *Find Your Courage* by Margie Warrell, and even *The Next Generation of Women Leaders* by Selena Rezvani all suggest a chasm between competence and confidence for females.

Where men assume they're ready for a new challenge when they're not, women are more likely to hold themselves back for fear that they're unprepared for the task in front of them. Similarly, men are more confident of themselves when they have no reason to be, where women lack confidence despite being fully qualified.

In both cases, stopping to objectively assess personal skills is one way to reduce the odds of over or underestimating personal leadership skills.

Avoiding the Dunning-Kruger Trap

Although the trap of Dunning-Kruger is easy to fall into, Webb took great pains to avoid it himself. That included:

Using 360-degree assessments to get feedback. Webb approached friends and colleagues who knew him in various capacities and asked for their frank evaluation of his skills. He wanted to know how others perceived him. He asked for examples to better understand what he was doing right and where he could improve.

Using psychometric instruments. While people around you can provide hard data about how you think and act, tools like those found in *First Break All the Rules: What the World's Greatest Managers Do Differently*, provide insights into your strengths and weaknesses from an internal perspective. The most valid and reliable instrument in predicting performance is the Hogan Personality Inventory. It is also more expensive and requires a certified coach to interpret the results. How do you instinctively react in certain situations, what environments bring out the best in you and which make you focus inward, what types of tasks do you gravitate towards—those are pieces of information others might not necessarily pick up on.

Comparing job requirements to personal skills. Using Webb's approach as a role model, a simple exercise you can do that will more clearly determine how well your skills line up with the requirements of the job you are considering, or are currently in, is to take two sheets of blank paper. Title one: "The job success requirements." Title the second: "My personal skills." On the first write out what the job entails and what types of skills and abilities will be key to performing well in that role. Then, on the other sheet, list your strengths.

Know thyself. That phrase is inscribed in stone on the temple of Apollo at Delphi. Great leaders know themselves well. In Webb's case, he went so far as to create an innovative organization designed to better run NASA. Understanding and accepting his own strengths and weaknesses and recognizing the intense pressure he was under to succeed at his job, he surrounded himself with complementary personalities and skillsets.

Forming the Triad

Having accepted a job at which he knew he was likely to fail, Webb took steps to compensate for his weaknesses using collaborative decision-making—essentially sharing decision-making responsibility and authority with others. He surrounded himself with leaders who had the experience he lacked and gave them the power to overrule him. He asked his predecessor at NASA, Hugh Dryden, to stay on and provide technical expertise, and then hired Robert Seamans, the former COO of RCA, who had the experience running an organization of that size that Webb lacked. Together, the three became known as The Triad, which was a new way of governing at the top.

The Triad was collaborative decision-making at its finest. For seven years, the three leaders—Webb, Dryden, and Seamans—made joint decisions. That meant that if two of the leaders were in favor of a course of action, their decision could overrule the lone man out. But each had his own sphere of excellence.

Hugh Dryden was "Dr. Science," Robert Seamans was "Mr. Inside," because he understood how organizations typically functioned internally, and Webb was "Mr. Outside," because he was plugged in to many governmental circles. He could work with Congress and the Executive Branch to align themselves with NASA when needed. Each role played to each individual's strengths and was a sign of how skilled a leader Webb was, to have figured that out and formed an organization to leverage those skills.

Although Seamans concurs that "each of us had different skills and responsibilities" as part of The Triad, along with the power to overrule each other 2:1, that was rarely necessary. "We convened to make key decisions that were usually unanimous," he says.[24]

The fact that Webb elected to take this approach to managing the organization is a testament to his leadership skills. He knew himself well enough to recognize he needed to supplement his own abilities and created an innovative organizational design to better run NASA.

The Rest of the Story

Even as the Hubble Space Telescope was being deployed, NASA was working on NGST, the "Next Generation Space Telescope." Hubble had been named after the astronomer Edwin Hubble who discovered that other galaxies exist besides the Milky Way. So, what to name the NGST? The James Webb Space Telescope name was selected because James Webb insisted to President Kennedy that the space program should not just aim at the moon, but "be balanced" and also serve to increase mankind's knowledge of the universe. That foresight to enlarge the scope of NASA eventually led to the NGST. The telescope's short name is just Webb.

How to Consistently Play to Your Strengths

Once you know your strengths and weaknesses, or the aspects of your job that aren't a good fit for your interests and ambitions, you can take steps to compensate using one of three primary tools:

- **Diversify.** Hugh Dryden, Bob Seamans, and James Webb couldn't have been more different from each other. Their diversity of education, experience, and interests provided what Webb called "a whole brain." We tend to hire people like ourselves. Webb had the awareness to not do that.

- **Delegate.** Find others equally or better qualified than you to whom you can hand off responsibilities. For example, I hate running meetings. I don't enjoy leading them, nor do I think I do a particularly good job, so I regularly ask others to take the lead in my place. I still attend and offer input, but I'm not the person driving the agenda. This also allows me to be a better listener. Our company runs much more smoothly as a result.

- **Partner with experts.** Just as academics often partner with fellow professors and scientists when undertaking research studies, effectively pooling their intellectual resources, you can increase your likelihood of success by identifying others with similar professional interests and ambitions—Webb's decision to share his leadership role with two experts is a perfect example. Look for ways to collaborate on projects. Working cooperatively can reduce your work load and improve the quality of outcome.

- **Hire smart people.** Most successful business owners understand that they will be much better served by hiring people smarter than they are than by hiring yes men and women. The key is figuring out what the different roles are to manage the organization effectively and then identifying talented candidates to fill those specific roles. Hiring skilled employees isn't enough on its own—they also need to be a good fit for the role they are being asked to fill.

As a leader, it's your responsibility to pull together the best team to achieve your organization's objectives. The most effective leaders define the various roles needed for the organization or business unit to be effective and then identify and hire the best candidates for each role. Simply hiring talented performers isn't enough—they need to be talented performers in their respective roles.

Leadership Insight

In most organizations there is a tricky balance of power between the field units and headquarters. I asked Doug Ward to review this chapter and he made the following comment: "There is no question in my mind that most old-time field center employees would rank Webb as the best of NASA administrators. He epitomized the field center view of an ideal administrator: handle dealings with congress and the White House, secure the funding, and leave the centers alone to manage their programs and work the technical details. Ed Kilgore headed the Office of Management at Headquarters during the two years I worked as an assistant on the administrator's staff in the Frosch/Lovelace administration and in the transition to the Beggs/Mark administration. On more than one occasion I heard Kilgore remind the administrator and other top managers that 'the strength of the agency is its field centers' with the implication headquarters should not attempt to micro-manage the centers." Webb knew how to balance the headquarters responsibility with the field need for autonomy.

One leader who was an expert at picking and choosing the best performers for each role on the team was Phil Jackson, former coach of the Chicago Bulls and the Los Angeles Lakers and widely considered to be the best professional basketball coach of all time, thanks to the eleven national championships his teams collectively earned.

Chris Chan of the *Bleacher Report*[25] broke down Jackson's coaching ability, pointing out:

> "The common theme with these guys [meaning players] is that they are specialists in a certain aspect of the game and are not a one-man team. Jackson utilized their strengths and put them in situations that would help the team the most."

He also understood that each player couldn't be dealt with the same way. Dennis Rodman, for example, was a unique case, but instead of kicking him off the team or coming down hard on him for his antics, Jackson came up with a compromise of sorts. The team needed Rodman's skills on the court, and Jackson didn't want other players believing they could be as undisciplined as Rodman off the court, so Jackson got the team's buy-in to allow for Rodman's poor behavior. In an interview with Dave Daniels,[26] he explained, "I went to the team and I said Dennis is gonna be late, I'm gonna fine him, but we can't act out of sorts with this and become childish because we have to make allowances for his behavior." The team was mature enough to let it slide, he says: "…the rest of the team didn't allow Rodman's lack of seriousness to stop them from 3-peating. Michael Jordan certainly wasn't going to let a goofball like Dennis derail what they had built in Chicago, and it is amazing that they were able to harness Rodman's rebounding, energy and defense without allowing his faults to appear on the court."

In the same way that Jackson found the best players for each position on the team, Webb did the same within NASA leadership. He knew he needed an aeronautical genius, so who better than a former MIT aeronautics professor—Seamans—to be involved in critical decisions? And he knew he needed someone familiar with the internal workings of government and NASA—his predecessor, Dryden, was his number one pick.

Although unorthodox at the time, Webb's decision to spread the decision-making authority across an odd number of leaders, to avoid stalemates, was innovative and effective. In forming The Triad, Webb put the most qualified person in each role, and ensured that no one individual would have more power than was warranted.

Does your organization have the best people in roles that leverage their strengths? If you could, would you move individuals into different roles? What do you do if you discover an employee is a bad fit for a role—are they given the opportunity to move into a role more suited to their skillset?

Leadership Experience

To be a better leader requires that you first take stock of your own strengths and weaknesses, so you can build a management team that shores up those weaknesses and makes the best use of your strengths. These resources can help you assess your skills:

- *The Leadership Challenge: How to Make Extraordinary Things Happen in Organizations*
- *The Hogan Personality Inventory*

To learn more about James Webb's leadership journey, check out these books:

- *The Man Who Ran the Moon: James E. Webb, NASA, and the Secret History of Project Apollo*
- *Powering Apollo: James E. Webb of NASA*

Now consider two questions:

- How accurately do you know your own strengths and weaknesses?
- How can you better utilize other people's talents so that you can play to your strengths?

CHAPTER 4

CHRISTOPHER KRAFT—
ORGANIZATIONAL LOCUS OF CONTROL

"Chris, you come up with a basic mission plan. You know, the bottom-line stuff on how we fly a man from a launch pad into space and back again. It would be good if you kept him alive."

—Chuck Matthews, chief of the Space Task Group[27]

Who's in charge? There is a natural tension that exists between units of an organization regarding which group has ultimate decision-making authority or control. Even in organizations with a strong hierarchy, there can be disagreement about who has the final say. Research and development and manufacturing tussle over which group has the final say over product features, just as manufacturing and sales have heated discussions over how products are made, and as upper and middle management negotiate for control over internal processes. The basic question is, who should be making what decision when? And there are differing viewpoints that come into play.

Christopher "Chris" Columbus Kraft, Jr. faced a new organization with an unclear reporting structure when he joined the Space Task Group (STG) in 1958. Their objective was putting a man into space. Exactly how needed to be determined.

Kraft thought he had nailed down the decision-making power and authority—locus of control—fairly early on. Or at least he established guidelines designed to limit disagreements.

After the Russians launched Sputnik, in 1958 President Eisenhower founded NASA (the National Aeronautics and Space Administration). It was a conglomeration of academic, military, and civilian organizations that were used to controlling their own operations. There was the Redstone Arsenal (military) in Alabama, Cape Canaveral (civilian) in Florida, the Langley Research Center (federal agency) in Virginia, and the Jet Propulsion Lab at CalTech (academic). Each had its own culture and way of doing things. Each had a unique way of resolving conflict and making decisions. Then added to that was the Manned Space

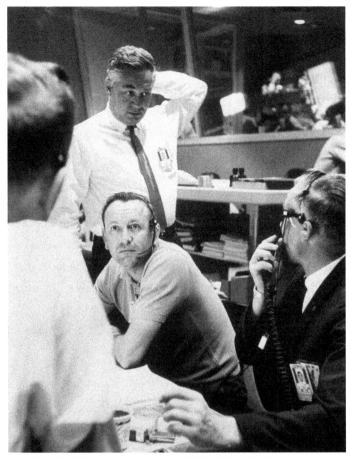

Chris Craft (seated) with Walter William (standing) at Mercury
Control Center, Cape Canaveral, Florida.
NASA Photo s63-07881

Flight Center, later renamed the Johnson Space Center
being built on pastureland in Texas. It was intent on
creating its own operational philosophy.

While all of these disparate units reported into
the Agency Headquarters in Washington, DC, it was

unclear initially which organization, if any, had the final say on different topics.

Leadership Insight

The term "locus of control" is used in many disciplines. Locus is a Latin word meaning "place" or "location." Control is from Anglo-French controller or to "exert authority." So, for our purposes as leaders, we use the term to describe where or by whom decisions are made. An interesting example of a physical place dictating is in the launch of a spacecraft. Launch control at Cape Kennedy has decision-making authority until the bottom of the rocket passes the highest point on the launch platform. At that moment authority transfers to Mission Control in Houston. So physical place and time clearly define who has locus of control.

Creating a Mission Plan

Job one. Kraft was first assigned the task of coming up with a mission plan—a plan for how the US could successfully get a man on the moon. He had no real experience in the field to prepare him for this task. That was by design. Bob Gilruth, the head of the country's manned space program, didn't want people on his team who had assumptions about what couldn't be done. So, he hired young people without biases like Kraft. They were moldable.

Given a blank sheet to work with—meaning nothing he had to include or that was off-limits—Kraft devised the idea of "Mission Control," a room where team members could see all the aspects of the space flight in real time in one place. The concept came out of his observations that other organizations coordinating large complex tasks have a centralized place to make decisions. Airports have control towers with traffic controllers perched high above the runways for a better vantage point, power plants have central offices, and that the air force has a central hub established for decision-making within the organization.

This was a new way of approaching the challenge of monitoring hundreds of aspects about a space mission. Historically, the process of coming up with a new approach or a new design went something like this:

- An RFP (request for proposal) is issued outlining what type of design is needed for, say, a plane.

- A company such as Boeing is given the contract and their team goes away and designs the plane to the specs they've proposed.

- Boeing tests its design and then delivers it to the army for testing.

- The army runs its own tests.

- If everything works as expected, the plane is put into production.

This standard military procurement process involved scattered decision-making, versus centralized. This decentralized approach took more time, in part because there were people at various junctures who had the power to overrule a decision.

Kraft learned first-hand the downsides of unclear decision-making authority.

Establishing a Locus of Control

During launches, Kraft, the flight director, was known as "Flight." Other members of the launch team were "Surgeon," "Retro," "FIDO," and "Capcom." Each was responsible for a portion of the larger task, from keeping the astronaut healthy during the flight to monitoring flight dynamics to staying in touch with the ship to bringing it back to earth. Although the team worked closely together, the ultimate decision-making rested with Flight. Kraft states in his book by the same name:

> "There's only one flight director. From the moment the mission starts until the moment the crew is safe on board a recovery ship, I'm in charge. I ask. I listen. I make decisions. No one can overrule me…They can fire me after it's over. But while the mission is under way, I'm Flight. And Flight is God."[28]

The reason for this clear delineation of power is to increase the odds that the individual who has the most information and expertise about a particular situation is in the power position. And Kraft was clearly the information hub, fed facts and figures by those in spoke roles. It placed all of the responsibility and all of the authority in one place.

However, the reason he insisted on the final word was due in part to a situation that occurred when John Glenn was in space. During his flight, the sensor on the rocket went off, suggesting that the heat shield was loose. Kraft saw the sensor warning and ordered the flight to continue. He was confident that the problem was with the sensor and not the heat shield itself.

Unfortunately, upper management got word of the sensor warning and disagreed with Kraft's opinion. After much discussion, hierarchy prevailed. Glenn was ordered to fire his retro-rockets early against Kraft's earlier instructions. Cutting the mission short was risky in itself but Glenn managed to reach earth safely. On inspection of the spacecraft, it was discovered that Kraft was correct—the sensor was loose, not the heat shield. Glenn had aborted his mission unnecessarily.

The lack of vertical alignment and clear decision-making authority on Glenn's flight needed to be corrected. From then on, Mission Control was in charge; Kraft had the final say during a flight. He was in control—or so he thought.

Mutiny on Board

Unfortunately, this was not the only time there was an issue with decision-making and control. Six years later, the disagreement wasn't from upper management at Johnson Space Center, but from 301 kilometers above the earth. During the Apollo 7 mission in 1968, with astronauts Wally Schirra, Donn Eisele, and Walter Cunningham orbiting Earth, there were a series of technical issues the men had to contend with. On top of that, all three came down with a head cold,[29] which was difficult to contend with in a pressurized cabin. They could blow their noses, but that was about it; not only was this painful but a ruptured ear drum was also a risk.

On this mission new safety procedures had been introduced in response to the death of Russian cosmonaut Vladimir Komarov the prior year due to depressurization on re-entry. The new rule was that astronauts had to put helmets and space suits on for the return flight.

Only Wally Schirra didn't want to. The problem was that once you put a helmet on, you can't clear your ears and are at risk of having an ear drum burst. The presence of a head cold made that risk much greater and Schirra didn't want to take it, he told Kraft so in no uncertain terms. This disagreement escalated into a full-on argument, with Kraft in Mission Control insisting that Schirra put his helmet on and Schirra, moving at 17,500 miles per hour, refusing.

Kraft was livid. There was nothing he could do to physically force Schirra to don his helmet and Schirra knew it. For Kraft, the issue was not about whether Schirra would suffer hearing loss as a result of his decision, but who had the power to make that decision in the first place. Kraft was supposed to have the final say and yet, clearly, his power was not absolute. He promised the astronauts that they would never fly again if they defied him. Schirra refused to put his helmet on and Kraft was true to his word; all three men were grounded for the remainder of their careers.

These examples illustrate that challenges to locus of control can come from many directions. In the case of John Glenn's flight, it was from higher up. With Apollo 7 it was from subordinates. There can also be confusion of authority between upstream and down-stream units or other functions.

Kraft needed to get this settled. He also took the rather extreme step of requesting an executive order from the president. The president agreed. Executive Order 14 CFR -1214.703 Chain of Command clearly stated that no one could override the flight director during an active flight—even the president of the United States.

Leadership Insight

Ethical behavior is a major concern in many areas of our lives. We cannot turn on the radio without hearing discussions about ethical dilemmas that face people in all sorts of situations.

As a leader you may be clear that you think certain types of behavior are wrong, but I'm sure you see that other people may hold passionate views on both sides of a right vs. wrong debate. Ethical behavior is about making moral judgments, about what is right and what is wrong, and then developing organizational values and codes of practice to implement those beliefs. You can ask anyone in Mission Control at NASA what the priorities are in making ethical decisions and they will quickly tell you, "Astronaut safety, vehicle safety, achieve the mission objectives."

Whenever you hear words like "good," "should," and "ought" in a conversation, you're probably in ethical territory. Do you have stated organizational values that will help decide what you "should" do?

When Decision-Making Power Needs to Shift

The head cold problem on Apollo 7 was child's play when compared to the complex challenges that arose on Apollo 11's trip to the moon in 1969. Eugene "Gene" Kranz was the flight director for the descent portion of the moon landing. After the lunar lander, named the Eagle, separated from the Command Module starting its downward path to the moon, things began to go wrong.

First, the ship headed to land in the wrong place— three miles down-range. Then the onboard computer failed. Data links were intermittent. The ship was low on fuel and the crew was concerned about whether they had enough to land. Add to that the fact that it took 2.5 seconds for a radio signal to reach the moon from earth, and another 2.5 to get back. Kranz quickly realized that he was a good five seconds behind the problems that were cropping up on board the Eagle. To get ahead of them, he needed to let the crew on the moon make decisions.

Kranz recalls that he "could feel the gravity of the decision-making moving from the earth to the moon." It's an almost poetic way for an engineer to describe his feelings. He could feel the locus of control moving from Houston Mission Control to Neil Armstrong on the moon. In a life-or-death situation, those closest to what's going on need to have more power, and Kranz recognized that.

The Rest of the Story

Differing organizational structures and culture can affect locus of control. Two of the NASA examples are differences between the Astronaut Corps and Mission Control, or the mission operations directorate. Traditionally they have been separate organizations with differing cultures. In 2014, Johnson Space Center Director Ellen Ochoa unified the fight crew and mission operations directorate into one organization—flight operations. This was part of her drive to advance human spaceflight by making the Johnson Space Center lean, agile, and adaptive to change. This particular reorganization can also be seen as a way to clarify the locus of control for decision-making. This flight operations emblem incorporates symbols from both of the previous organizations.

This shift of power from management to customer-facing employees also happens in the private sector. At Florida Power & Light Company (FPL), for example, the company knows it's going to get hit with hurricanes each year. That's a given based on its geography and service area. And when hurricanes hit, it's hard to stay on top of the repairs to be made. The executives at Florida Power understand that the locus of control for decision—making has to change when the stress of a hurricane hits.

So, what happens when a hurricane strikes is that FPL's traditional hierarchy gets turned on its head.

Instead of line technicians reporting up the chain of command, they are the ones in charge during times of crisis, driving the allocation of resources and decisions that need to be made. They're closer to the situation—or ahead of it—whereas senior management can only wait for status reports, much like Kranz did. During hurricanes, many non-critical functions, managers, and even executives move into support roles. I know of a senior learning executive whose job becomes checking on the line technicians' families, to ensure their safety and comfort while the linemen handle the business.

Leadership Insight

Another factor to consider when defining locus of control is domain knowledge. Domain knowledge is expertise in a specific specialized field or discipline; IT is a common example. Most leaders lack extensive domain knowledge of computers and software engineering. Therefore, it's wise to move the locus of control for those decisions to specialists. In the Florida Power & Light example, technicians not only have more awareness of the problems on the ground, but they also have superior domain knowledge. It makes sense on both counts to empower them to make critical decisions.

There can also be a middle ground for leaders. You may keep the decision-making but call upon others with unique domains of knowledge for advice. During World

War II, Winston Churchill rode the underground or subway to understand the views of the common man. He also called upon specialists in various military and technical fields. But the locus of control remained with him.

What's critical within NASA, at Florida Power & Light, and within your organization, is knowing who, when, and where decisions are made. Even when you plan carefully as Chris Kraft did, there can still be confusion or even disagreements. As leaders we must plan carefully and be ready to adjust.

Leadership Experience

Who has the final say? And does that power shift in certain situations? What are they? The most effective organizations understand that decision-making power isn't stationary—it moves and evolves. But that movement should be a conscious transition.

Other ways to decide who has the locus of control in particular situations might include:

- Where might there be confusion over who is the final arbiter to make decisions in your organization?

- What criteria or guiding principles should be used to decide where the locus of control should reside; i.e. who is closest to the problem, who knows the most (domains of knowledge), who is held responsible if something goes wrong?

Looking to the future, consider thinking about how best to develop the next generation of decision-makers, such as:

- Who could move into a decision-making role?

- What kind of experiences should they have to develop that skill?

- Are there opportunities now to develop people?

- Do we have tactics, such as personal signals, to help employees surreptitiously ask for help on-the-spot?

CHAPTER 5

WERNHER VON BRAUN— RENAISSANCE LEADERSHIP

"As a successful scientist moves up the ladder, he becomes more of a specialist, his field of interest usually narrows, and he gets to know more and more about less and less. As a successful manager moves up the ladder, his interests must broaden. Conversely, it seems that he must know less and less about more and more."

—Wernher von Braun[30]

The most successful managers in modern organizations are T-shaped. That is, they have deep expertise in one area *and* they have a working knowledge of other organizational functions; they are both specialists and generalists simultaneously. Wernher von Braun was a T-shaped manager. He had a doctorate in physics and of course had a deep understanding of rocketry as evidenced by his thesis title "About Combustion Tests." But his rapid rise from junior engineer to Direktor at Peenemünde in Germany was because of his broad range of management skills. Von Braun arrived in the US as a T-shaped manager. He continued to hone his abilities once he was on Uncle Sam's payroll. He grew in his understanding of other functions, such as logistics, finance, and human resources. He saw how the combination of these functions impacts an organization's success.

The term "T-shaped" doesn't only refer to an individual's knowledge. The vertical bar of the T does represent the depth of skill in a particular area or domain of knowledge. But the horizontal bar represents both knowledge and the person's ability to collaborate and apply their thinking across disciplines. It's this ability to collaborate that is the essence of the success of T-shaped leaders.

The earliest reference to T-shaped managers was by David Guest "The hunt is on for the Renaissance Man of computing," *The Independent* (London), September 17, 1991. But Tim Brown, the CEO of IDEO and author of the book *Change by Design* is credited with spreading the idea in management circles.[31]

Brown emphasized personal attributes as a primary dimension of the horizontal bar. In an interview in

Von Braun reads a book on a break during the launch of
Apollo Mission A-101. NASA Photo 9605272

Chief Executive magazine, he described the horizontal bar this way.

"The horizontal stroke of the 'T' is the disposition for collaboration across disciplines. It is composed of two things. First, empathy. It's important because it allows people to imagine the problem from another perspective—to stand in somebody else's shoes. Second, they tend to get very enthusiastic about other people's disciplines, to the point that they may actually start to practice them. T-shaped people have both depth and breadth in their skills."[32]

The Antidote to Specialization

Why is this emphasis on T-shaped management happening now? The answer is that we live in a world of growing specialization. Specialization began in manufacturing to improve efficiency and quality. But it's gone way beyond that into all facets of large organizations. For example: the number of specialties approved by the Association of American Medical Colleges grew from thirty-four in 1975 to 131 today.[33] That's an increase of almost four hundred percent. That same phenomenon is happening in other fields from engineers to consultants. The work world is dividing like cells. Organizations need leaders who understand the strengths of specialization but who can also bring this fragmented workforce together.

So, we also see T-shaped leaders as integrators, bringing the different parts of an organization together.

Cook often uses the term "facilitator" to describe this horizontal role.

Von Braun was especially skilled at this type of cross-functional and cross-organizational facilitation. He leveraged his position to move his colleagues into other organizations and positions of responsibility. For example, his longtime collaborator in Germany, Kurt Debus became the Center Director at Cape Canaveral. By pushing his best people into other organizations, he also extended his own network. These inroads improved cooperation between the NASA centers and between functions. And just as he did his best to support the promotion and career growth of employees up and out of his organization, he also welcomed new employees into his organization in Huntsville. That's how von Braun's own functional knowledge and connections continued to expand throughout his career.

The Rest of the Story

David Guest is an IT analyst and an author. He saw the growth of specialization in IT as a hindrance to performance. In addition to coining the term T-shaped manager, he also described this new type of leader as a "hybrid" manager and as a Renaissance leader. "The hunt for a new breed of computer manager is on. The British Computer Society, in a controversial report published last year, described the quarry as a 'hybrid' manager who would combine business expertise with IT skills. The hybrid manager would be distinguished by his or her ability to relate to 'the broad picture' and to people, understanding their motivation and aspirations; he or she would also be energetic, intuitive, a good listener, and would have an unusual set of interests."

Note that he describes the characteristics of these hybrid managers in terms of personal attributes and not just areas of functional knowledge.

Advantages of T-Shaped Organizations

Von Braun is best known for creating the world's most powerful rocket—the Saturn V. But he should also be recognized for the organization he built through T-shaped management. That organization had three notable attributes.

Improved communication and collaboration—T-shaped leaders have a superior grasp of how the horizontal functions of an organization fit together. They tend to have a greater appreciation of the different kinds of work these units perform. In turn, they demand more sharing and partnering to achieve superior solutions to problems.

Enhanced flexibility—T-shaped leaders tend to use leadership teams for more work and to use those teams more effectively. Over time these teams become more self-organizing and more adaptable to change.

Silos and bottle necks—By emphasizing the communication and collective problem-solving across functions, the bottlenecks of workflow tend to lessen, and sub optimization or silo mentality weakens.

Problem-solving Prowess

T-shaped managers tend to be more adept at figuring out what problem they need to solve and then developing more creative and innovative ways of dealing with them. We all have our own filters driven by our experience and training. We tend to see the world through those filters. Engineers tend to see the world as a set of math problems. HR professionals see people issues. Many managers have these types of cognitive bias and, as a result, misdiagnose the problem or come up with a weak solution. Because T-shaped managers can more readily see a problem from different perspectives, they are better able to diagnose the problem correctly. This, in turn, leads to better, or at least more effective, solutions.

Across the board, Von Braun was very good at quickly identifying the type of problem he was facing. Of course, many were technical, but as you look at his history, the major difficulties he faced were more business and political in nature. Von Braun the physicist became adept at solving these different types of problems, but more so utilizing the strengths of others. Von Braun put it this way in 1962.

"A team is made up of many individuals. The more individualistic, the better. When putting a team together, the manager should not try to find people whom he can outsmart, but people who are smarter than he is in their particular fields. The smarter the people at the working level are, the better the team. I think nothing hurts a team effort more—and the exploration of space is the greatest of team efforts—than what you might call the 'pappy knows best' attitude on the part of top management. Pappy just doesn't always know what is best. He gets the best answers if he asks the man who is to do the job."[34]

Targeted Integration

We should not think that developing T-shaped leaders is the panacea for all horizontal alignment issues. The goal of cross-functional integration is not integration, but improved business results. Because they are specialists themselves, T-shaped managers should try to identify when specialization is needed and when a more integrated approach is best. Therefore, we should carefully select when we use horizontal skills to improve performance.

A colleague of mine is a partner in a thirty-person consulting firm. The company has been very successful for almost thirty years. They hired a general manager to run the business and to free up the partners for other work. The company had had three standing governance boards for many years. The new general manager created eighteen new committees and councils to address various issues. As business results started to dip, the partners realized that over-collaboration was one of the causes. The partners and the general manager went through the different committees to determine which were contributing to business growth and which were not.

Leaders need to be wary of over-using either specialization or integration. We should carefully select which projects could benefit from collaboration and which will not. Part of that selection should include identifying the barriers to collaboration. These barriers could be resources, structure, or other organizational characteristics. Sometimes they relate more to the people involved or past histories of attempts to collaborate.

Leadership Insight

Harv Hartman was responsible for Human Resources at Johnson Space Center for many years and worked with Wernher and his team. One of the 126 scientists who came over to the US from Germany with von Braun had become frustrated with the inordinate number of salary grades in NASA. The scientist complained to Harv in front of von Braun, "You Americans have way too many levels! In Germany, we only had six." Von Braun put his hands on his colleague's shoulder and reminded him, "We aren't in Germany anymore."

Harv says that von Braun picked his battles wisely.

Developing T-shaped Leaders

Some people grow into T-shaped managers naturally. Chris More wrote a wonderful article about his life "I am T-shaped. Are you too? Learn from my story."[35] In that story, he describes how in his childhood he loved art and developed a good hand with drawing. In his teen years he became interested in a variety of subjects and people. In this excerpt he describes the social side of becoming a T-shaped person.

"A common question kids would ask each other is 'Who is your best friend?' ... My default answer for the best friend question was always 'I have many best friends.' What I meant was that I had a lot of different interests as a teenager, from technology, automotive racing, cars, art, sports, and electronics. With each of my interests, I had a different set of friends and a best friend related to that topic. Instead of just one set of friends, I had multiple pyramids of people related to each of my interest areas. I quickly learned that I was pretty unique with my friend setup, because in each of those topical friend groups, the kids didn't really engage with other groups of kids. This became pretty apparent, for example, when my computer best friend was talking bad about another kid who happened to be my car stereo best friend. This was often a hard line to walk.

"Even though I had many friends and multiple interests, I felt like I was almost a different person with each group of people. Each group had unique norms and inside jokes that outsiders wouldn't really understand. This was pretty challenging to 'fit in' with each group and feel like you are part of the tribe, but that's who I was, thus I kept doing it over and over."

More's story illustrates two points. First, some people naturally gain a breadth of knowledge simply because they are interested in many things. They don't work at it. It just happens. The second aspect is the social dimension—the different norms and languages. If we're not naturally a Chris More, how can we develop ourselves and others as T-shaped leaders?

A good first step is to identify the areas where you have expertise and those areas where you may be lacking. This can be as sophisticated as competency mapping or as simple as reflecting on our strengths and experience.

One of the best ways of learning is to work side-by-side with someone else. Von Braun used this approach at all levels. He not only embraced moving people within NASA, but also sought to involve people from academia and commercial contractors in the work.

Von Braun was a champion of learning. Even as a prisoner of war he was an avid reader and formed learning groups to teach his engineers and scientists cross-functional knowledge. He also used small teams of diverse backgrounds to solve problems together.

Von Braun modeled the way for other leaders. One method Von Braun used was weekly work summaries. He had each of his direct reports write a one-page summary of their unit's work each Friday. Over the weekend Von Braun would make notations and write questions on these "one-pagers." On Mondays he had the sheets with his comments collated and distributed back out to everyone. These summaries became important sources for horizontal information sharing.

Von Braun recognized the behavioral side of having T-shaped managers. He tailored the recognition and reward systems available to him to deemphasize individual accomplishment and emphasize collaboration. This same emphasis applied to promotion.

He looked for these characteristics in his hiring.

"Now the ideal scientist-manager of a complex research and development project must broaden his interests in width and depth. He needs a broad background and experience in Mathematics, Chemistry, Physics, and Engineering. He must understand the relationships among the various disciplines, and their interface in applications to his project. Each specialist sitting around the table must feel that the director understands the problems in his particular field. The director must be able to discuss the problem in the language of that discipline."[36]

T-shaped because of necessity

I have a personal story. Our daughter Shelby was born with multiple disabilities. Neither my wife Margaret or I were prepared. As we realized the extent of Shelby's medical disorders, my wife started to prepare herself for the additional roles of nurse, physical therapist, advocate, and education specialist. She became so adept with the medical terminology that while we were waiting for some test results, a physician asked her where she did her residency. We still laugh at that as Margaret's degree is in marketing. I guess she sold the doctors.

The World is Flat

David Friedman points out in his book *The World is Flat* that the globalization of business demands that the workforce and its leaders need to be more adaptable. As we work across national boundaries and more importantly across cultures, the need to have leaders who are both deep and broad is increasing.

The *Harvard Business Review* article "What is a Global Manager?" summarized it this way.

"As a first step, senior executives can identify those in the organization with the potential for developing the skills and perspectives demanded of global managers. Such individuals must have a broad, nonparochial view of the company and its operations yet a deep understanding of their own business, country, or functional tasks. Obviously, even many otherwise talented managers in an organization aren't capable of such a combination of flexibility and commitment to specific interests, especially when it comes to cross-border coordination and integration."[37]

All business takes place within a social and political ecosystem. That ecosystem is always changing. Tariffs, taxes, labor disputes, consumer preferences, legal ruling, and social causes are just a few of the current forces affecting businesses. Von Braun said, "No top research manager today can ignore the economic, political, and even the social interface of huge national programs. He can't hold himself aloof from politics and say he doesn't care for it. It matters."[38]

So, the need for T-shaped leaders like Von Braun is increasing. Consider ways you can become more t-shaped such as:

- Gain deeper mastery in one skill or knowledge domain. Don't be a "hyphen" flitting from one thing to the next. Tim Brown describes these people as having empty experiences. If you want to make a dent in the world, you have to become an expert with deep knowledge in a specific area.

- Remain curious. While you're focusing on your primary skill, don't lose your curiosity for other disciplines and/or parts of your business. If you're in R&D, go for a beer with someone from sales—you could be surprised by what you learn.

- Read more to connect more dots. Renaissance thinkers read a lot.

- Focus on showing empathy to become a better problem solver. According to Tim Brown, empathy is an important characteristic to foster if you want to become a T-shaped person. "It's important because it allows people to imagine the problem from another perspective—to stand in somebody else's shoes. Second, they tend to get very enthusiastic about other people's disciplines, to the point that they may actually start to practice them,"

Leadership Experience

- Assess yourself on the two dimensions of the T.

- How could you find others to help you be more broad in your ability to collaborate?

CHAPTER 6
HIDDEN FIGURES — UNDERSTANDING SOCIAL CAPITAL

"You are the sum total of the people you meet and interact with in the world. Whether it's your family, peers, or co-workers, the opportunities you have and the things that you learn all come through doors that other people open for you."[39]

—Tanner Colby, *Some of My Best Friends Are Black: The Strange Story of Integration in America*

The book *Hidden Figures* showcases the important work that a group of African-American women did to support the American manned space program in the 1960s. The biographical text focuses on the lives of three women: Katherine Goble Johnson, Dorothy Vaughan, and Mary Jackson. All three were mathematicians, also known as "human computers," working to overcome discrimination as women and as African-Americans. Although the great divide between White and Black professionals working side-by-side was the dramatic backdrop, social capital was an underlying leadership theme.

It's who you know. Social capital is the network of people we are connected to that enables us to function in society and, eventually, to succeed. People who grow up in privilege have social relationships that allow them to succeed more readily or easily than those who are not connected to that network. Social connections are social capital—an asset that can be leveraged and traded for personal and professional gain.

Social capital is an aspect of cultural capital, which is a more macro view of your social standing. Cultural capital includes where you grew up, the schools you attended, how you behave, the language you use—even the accent you have. All of those facets of your life contribute to your persona and determine how easily you can get ahead.

There are also symbols of cultural capital that we can use to assert our social standing.

Leveraging Cultural Capital

In one of the early scenes in the movie *Hidden Figures*, a police car pulls up behind a broken-down car with the three African-American women in it. The women are nervous, not sure how they'll be treated by the White officer. With a scowl he asks what the women are doing on the road. They nervously explain that the car broke down.

When the officer asks where they're headed and one of the women pulls out her NASA badge—a symbol of cultural capital—the whole demeanor of the police officer changes. His attitude immediately shifts from suspicion to admiration.

"Can I give you an escort?" he asks, once they get the car running again. Shocked, the women gratefully accept the offer.

The enhanced social capital that the NASA badge provided the three contract employees is similar to the social capital Jim Webb acquired solely by virtue of the family he was born into. Webb's parents were teachers who valued intellectual achievement. They exposed him to culture and the arts. He himself was well-educated and informed, allowing him to converse with colleagues who had attended Ivy League universities and to earn their respect.

He also served in the Marine Corps during World War II, another social connection that earned him respect and admiration in general society. Webb's military service also plugged him into another broader social network that would be good for his career.

His networks—thanks to his parents, high school and college schooling, his work in government, and his military service—all served to greatly enhance Webb's social capital.

In a similar manner, Katherine Johnson was able to succeed because of the same factors. Johnson's impressive intelligence was obvious as a child. She was fascinated with numbers and started high school at age ten. Katherine lived in White Sulphur Springs, West Virginia, and the school for African-Americans stopped at the eighth grade. Katherine's father, Joshua, was determined to give his children the opportunities he never had, so he rented a house 120 miles away in Institute, West Virginia. There, Blacks could pursue an education past the eighth grade, through high school. He drove back and forth to White Sulphur Springs

Langley Research Center. Seated from the left: Katherine Johnson, Lawrence Brown, and J Norwood Evans. Standing from the left: John Cox and Edward Maher. NASA Photo LRC-1965-B701_P-02289

from his job at a hotel for eight years. At the school in Institute, Katherine found teachers, administrators, and others who believed in her. She proved to be so smart that she skipped several grades, graduating from high school at age fourteen and from West Virginia State College at eighteen.

Both James Webb's and Katherine Johnson's success can be at least partially traced back to the social networks they had through their families, schools, and workplaces. They had people in positions of power who helped them.

The Rest of the Story

While the scene showing Al Harrison angrily knocking down a "Colored Bathroom" sign was dramatic, it actually never happened. That's because when NASA was created in 1958, its charter prohibited that kind of segregation. NASA never had separate bathrooms for Blacks.

Did Katherine Johnson feel the segregation of the outside world while working at NASA?

No. "I didn't feel the segregation at NASA, because everybody there was doing research," says the real Katherine G. Johnson. "You had a mission and you worked on it, and it was important to you to do your job... and play bridge at lunch. I didn't feel any segregation. I knew it was there, but I didn't feel it." Even though much of the racism coming from Katherine's coworkers in the movie is exaggerated (in real life she claimed to be treated as a peer), the movie's depiction of state laws regarding the use of separate bathrooms and buses was very real. African-American computers had also been put in the segregated west section of the Langley campus and were dubbed the "West Computers." —*WHROTV interview*[40]

Building Social Capital

Employees and colleagues come to us with different amounts of social capital. As leaders we can assess who has had an advantage and who may need some assistance in gaining more social capital to even the playing field. By virtue of our position of power, leaders can "grease the skids," as they say, to propel an employee's career along faster or farther. Some of the ways leaders can help junior employees amass more social capital include:

- **Fitting in.** Having access to higher-level leaders is an advantage, but unless you can connect with them socially, you'll still be on the outside looking in. Leaders can provide access and feedback. Access can be as literal as being invited to certain meetings or events. Or it can be sharing insights on how the organization functions and the unwritten rules. That includes feedback on how you behave, topics to discuss, and other suggestions that can help you fit in more easily.

- **Building a network.** Introductions to others within your organization or within your community can help immensely. "Being connected" is a valuable asset that only occurs when you're plugged in to social circles.

- **Giving exposure.** Making introductions helps make others aware of you, but until you have the opportunity to show what you know, or what you can accomplish, you may be relegated to the sidelines. Leaders can offer high profile assignments, provide public praise for a job well done, and mentor employees regarding ways to improve their visibility within the organization, to gain additional social capital.

- **Bringing them along.** It's one thing to have your boss introduce you to their fellow managers at a local Rotary meeting and something else to have your boss invite you to attend a private executive roundtable discussion next month. Both situations are useful, but when a leader invites you to tag along to an event, the smart response is always "yes." Because at those events, you'll be privy to information you won't hear anywhere else. And you'll have aligned yourself with your boss, which gives you even more social capital by virtue of his position.

Leaders can also help with cultural capital, with changing the way the organization is run. In the movie,

Al Harrison takes many steps to enhance Katherine Johnson's social capital within NASA.

In one scene in the movie, Johnson asks to be admitted to the Pentagon Briefings so that her work wouldn't be out of date as soon as she began work on it. But she gets pushback from Paul Stafford, who doesn't believe she belongs in the meeting, nor that she has the right to be there. Johnson appeals to Harrison's sense of what's fair and what's efficient:

Paul Stafford: "Pentagon Briefings are not for civilians. It requires the highest clearance."

Katherine Johnson: "I feel like I'm the best person to present my calculations, Mr. Harrison."

Al Harrison: "You're not going to let this go. Are you?"

Katherine Johnson: "No, sir."

Paul Stafford: "And she's a woman. There's no protocol for a woman attending."

Al Harrison: "Okay, I get that part, Paul. But within these walls, who makes the rules?"

Katherine Johnson: "You, sir. You're the boss. You just have to act like one."

And he does, inviting her into the room. With that decision, Harrison elevates Johnson's cultural capital, bringing her into the fold of the top-secret Pentagon meetings. She's one of them.

But he takes it a step beyond merely introducing her to the network seated at the conference table. When there is a question about the size of the landing zone and how they can possibly know where the astronaut will land in the ocean, Johnson is called on to do some calculations.

Al Harrison: "Have a go at it?"

Johnson meekly takes the chalk he extends to her— the symbolic passing of the baton—and walks slowly to the front of the room, all eyes on her. She is now in the position of power—quite literally, but it's also an audition to see if she deserves that social power. She is standing at the chalkboard while they are seated behind her, watching her every calculation. They are totally reliant on her to calculate the exact landing zone.

Scenes like these in the movie, though short, illustrate how social and cultural capital work and how leaders can help others enhance theirs.

The Rest of the Story

The film primarily centers in on John Glenn's 1962 flight as the first American to orbit Earth. Hollywood does make it dramatic. Katherine Johnson's main job in the lead-up and during the mission was to double-check and reverse engineer the newly-installed IBM 7090s trajectory calculations.

A false warning light did force the mission to end early. NASA records show that John Glenn did request that Johnson specifically check and confirm trajectories that the IBM mainframe calculated. As Shetterly wrote in her book and explained in an NPR interview,[41] Glenn did not completely trust the new computer. He did ask the flight engineers to "get the girl to check the numbers... If she says the numbers are good... I'm ready to go."

Offering Guidance

Sometimes being the leader can be uncomfortable, especially when it becomes obvious you need to address a sensitive subject, such as how someone dresses.

In my first management job, one of my responsibilities was overseeing the main lobby at IBM-Boulder, including hiring. We needed a summer intern to fill in for the receptionist. The college student we hired fit the stereotypical role well. That is, she was friendly, attractive, and approachable. She had also been Miss Colorado.

The first week of work, everything went well. She caught on quickly and did a great job.

But as the weeks wore on, I noticed her attire got more and more bizarre. The week I saw her in flip flops one day and an evening gown the next forced me to do something. It was extremely awkward.

I brought her into my office. "I need to talk to you about the dress code," I told her. She became distressed.

"We don't have a dress code, but you need to change."
She explained to me that she didn't want to be seen
in the same outfit twice.

"What should I wear?" she asked me.

"Look at what successful women here wear and
copy them. If you do that, you'll fit right in at IBM,"
I reassured her. "You don't want people to notice your
clothes, you want them to notice your performance,"
I explained. I was trying to help her to fit in.

She got it. While I saw one particular brown pant-
suit many times that summer, she looked like an IBMer.
From then on, no one commented on her clothes, only
on what a good job she was doing. Years later she ended
up as a software engineer for the City of Denver.

I was lucky to face this kind of obvious social
challenge as a new manager. While these types of
conversations are uncomfortable for everyone involved,
they are critical for the employee in need of guidance
and help in our complex social systems. By offering
insights and feedback, leaders can help employees be
even more successful, and they can help others acquire
more social capital.

Advising someone on dress code is a very simple
example. Let's go a little deeper. There are two basic ways
to measure social capital. First is the volume or number
of contacts in your network. Second is the strength of the
connection to each of those network ties. In his book, *The
Tipping Point*, Malcolm Gladwell describes the benefits
of both a large number of "loose ties and a small number
of strong ties." A leader with lots of loose ties can tap

his or her network to locate important information or important decision-makers. A leader with a small number of strong relationships can create more trust and make larger requests of those in his or her network.

People often picture companies as organization charts. But, in fact, they are more like spiderwebs with loose ties and strong ties. Let's say you have a legal or a finance question. It's one thing to know where those departments report. It's a very different thing to say I know someone I can call in legal to get some help, but I don't know anyone in finance. Leaders need these networks to get things done. And you can use them to help your team make even more connections.

This sociogram is a graphical representation to illustrate people's connections. You may want to sketch out your connections to more easily see how strong they are and where you may have gaps.

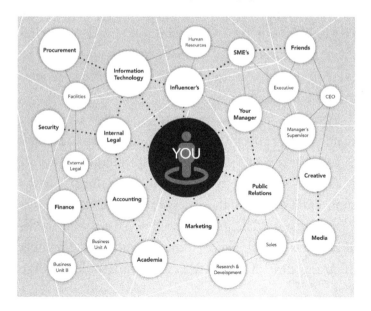

Becoming Attuned to Signals You're Sending

In addition to networks and dress codes, there are plenty of other unwritten rules of work of which people lacking in social capital may not be aware. Leaders have an opportunity to help team members gain cultural and social capital by making them aware of how they're presenting themselves.

Employees may need coaching in any number of areas that are impacting their ability to be promoted. These include:

- **Speech.** How employees express themselves and the language they use at work can color how they are perceived by others. Every organization has its own lexicon and way of communicating. In particular, people new to an organization may need help adjusting their communication style. Writing a good business letter is very different from writing a dissertation.

- **Behavior.** Sometimes it's not the words used but the conversations themselves that occur at work that can be career-damaging. Every organization has behaviors you just don't do or things "we don't talk about."

- **Hierarchy.** Some organizations are egalitarian and others are hierarchical. Understanding the social hierarchy, if any, is critical to being accepted. This is particularly true when working cross-culturally, where customs and cultural norms may differ.

- **Time orientation.** The connection of the past with the current actions and challenges can vary greatly. Some organizations are steeped in tradition and honor their past as a guide to making decisions about the future. Other organizational cultures value change and seek rapid adaption and innovation.

- **Hero or team.** Some organizational cultures have a strong preference for achievement, heroism, and assertiveness. Conflict is viewed as natural and good. Other organizations place a preference for cooperation, modesty, and being part of the team. Conflict is carefully controlled and even seen as negative.

Leaders are in an excellent position to offer advice, coaching, and refer employees to outside resources or courses, if needed, to shore up the areas they're weak in.

Basically, it all comes down to fitting in and not doing anything that distracts those around you.

Leadership Insight

One way to ensure you're helping yourself or others to fit into the organizational culture is to pretend you are an anthropologist. Try to be objective and observe your organization as though you are looking at it for the first time.

Look at artifacts and space. What do they say to you? Are they warm and inviting or sterile? Does the space invite collaboration or imply hierarchy? What's on people's desks and hanging on the walls? Watch for how emotions are displayed. Emotions can indicate values. Examine conflicts closely; are they engaged, friendly, morose, tense?

How do people interact with each other? How would you describe to someone else how senior leaders interact with middle managers or employees? What don't you see or hear? What subjects or behaviors appear to be taboo? What are the underlying assumptions that may be guiding people's interactions?

As Yogi Berra famously said, "You can observe a lot just by watching."

Leadership Experience

Some of us are lucky. We had parents like Katherine Johnson's or James Webb's who provided us with ways to gain social capital and make our way in the world. Some people build their social capital naturally and use it to accomplish goals without thinking about it. But many people fail to recognize how their lack of social capital inhibits their ability to get work done and progress in their careers.

As leaders we have a dual responsibility: to manage our own social capital and to help others gain and use social capital more effectively. To improve your use of social capital, it is helpful to examine your network of connections with the following questions in mind:

- Are there holes in my network that I need to fill?

- Do I need to make my "loose network" larger or focus on making a few key relationships much stronger?

- How am I helping others build their networks?

- How can I open my network to help others gain more social capital?

- Where can I generate reciprocity to strengthen ties with others?

CHAPTER 7

GLYNN LUNNEY — SCALES OF RECIPROCITY

"Our leadership trusted us and gave us room
to do our jobs. In return, we gave them our
very best efforts and loyalty."

—Glynn Lunney

It's not about the money. NASA's finest engineers
could certainly have made more money working in
the private sector; government pay is not known for
being lucrative. But many stayed because they liked the
work they did and liked the people they worked with.
That is, as they weighed what they were expected to

give of their expertise and what they received in return from their job, they were more than satisfied with the trade—with the balance.

One of the "fathers of space flight," Glynn Lunney, was keenly aware of this balance, also known as the scales of reciprocity. As individual contributor, manager, and flight director, he did his best to keep the internal and external scales on an even keel. Some managers only concern themselves with external scales—whether their contributions would be more richly rewarded elsewhere versus at their current employer. But the internal scales that have a greater impact on work teams, because they have to do with the work environment, relationships with co-workers, recognition, and compensation, among other considerations.

Leaders have more control over the internal scales, Lunney recognized. That is one factor that made him a boss his employees didn't want to leave.

Glynn Lunney at his console in the Mission Control Center, Houston. NASA Photo s65-61502

A Leader's Origins

Perhaps because he grew up in a Pennsylvania coal-mining town, where income was presumably hard-earned, Lunney valued relationships over money. After graduating from Scranton Preparatory School, he headed to the University of Scranton to study engineering.

He had always been fascinated with flight, and his father, a welder and former miner, encouraged him to strive for a life beyond the mines. After two years, Lunney transferred to the University of Detroit to participate in a co-op program with the Lewis (now Glenn) Research Center in Ohio, which was part of the National Advisory Committee for Aeronautics (NACA). He graduated in 1958 with a degree in aeronautical engineering and was hired by NACA to conduct research in aerospace dynamics.

He didn't stay there long, however, choosing to transfer to Langley to become part of the original team of thirty-five who formed the Space Task Group's (STG) Flight Dynamics Office.

These formative years laid the foundation for Lunney's leadership philosophy. In his book *Highways into Space*, Lunney speaks about his first days at the Flight Dynamics Branch:

> "This was a 'Band of Brothers' in the best tradition of that honored term. Some of the magic was the sense of coming together to do something really

big, something that had never been done before. Some of it was the mutual reliance of all of these men on each other."[42]

These notions of mutual reliance and reciprocity would grow as Lunney's career progressed. Initially the mutual reliance was based in the needs of a small team challenged with monumental tasks of returning a spaceship safely back to earth. As Lunney moved up to become a flight director with broader responsibilities, these notions would become a management philosophy.

Management by Respect

Lunney credits Bob Gilruth and Chris Kraft with creating a new management style, which became casually known as "management by respect."[43]

Unlike other supervisors and leaders who manage by intimidation or by consensus or by walking around, Lunney says NASA leaders managed through trust and respect for those around them. Despite the fact that many of their subordinates were barely out of college, Gilruth et al. held them in high regard. By demonstrating respect for team members when they might not have otherwise received it, Lunney suggests, STG leaders earned the life-long loyalty and admiration of their direct reports.

Lunney describes the leadership environment[44] in which the team worked:

"We operated on a balanced chemical equation where they gave us trust and the stuff to do the job—support—and they did that every day. And we gave them back loyalty and the best job we could do. And you know, it was perfectly balanced. Because the trust continued and our sense of obligation for having been given that trust increased our incentive to perform well…that's as good an equation for leadership as you can get."

That sense of balance was an essential ingredient to the success of the Apollo program. The scales of respect and trust given by leaders were always evenly balanced with the personal effort and dedication of the NASA engineers. The more respect and appreciation shown by leadership, the harder the engineers worked to ensure the success of the mission. As Lunney says, there was a sense of "obligation," of payback, for the respect they were shown.

This is the essence of reciprocity—giving as much of yourself as you've received in exchange from your boss or your employer for your expertise and work ethic. Every relationship, personal and professional, has an element of reciprocity.

Currencies

When we think of exchanges of value, we naturally think of currencies. Employers ask, "What is your current annual salary?" Employees ask, "What does the position pay?" We ask about money. However, there are many other forms of value and, thus, other forms of currency. We can take a page from the Harvard Negotiations Project and the work done by professors William Ury and Roger Fisher. They identify many forms of alternate currencies which we can summarize into two types: alternative currencies and elegant currencies.

Alternative currencies are anything, other than money, that has value to you or others with whom you work. What are those things? A survey by Boston Consulting Group (BCG)[45] polled more than 200,000 employees around the world to create a definitive list of the top ten factors that people want from their work.[46] They found that employees value the following (in order of importance):

1. Appreciation for their work

2. Good relationships with colleagues

3. Good work-life balance

4. Good relationships with superiors

5. Company's financial stability

6. Learning and career development

7. Job security

8. Attractive fixed salary

9. Interesting job content

10. Company values

Only two of the ten factors are related to money. The other eight are alternative currencies. Those factors have value. Now look at this list again and ask yourself, "How many of these ten factors can I strongly influence for my subordinates?"

There is a subset of this list of alternate currencies that are described as "elegant currencies."

Elegant currencies are alternative currencies that have high value to the receiving party, and low cost (or no cost) to the giver. For example, appreciation and good relations with colleagues don't necessarily cost any money and they are under the direct control or at least influence of leaders.

Let's go back to Glynn Lunney's quote at the beginning of this chapter. "Our leadership trusted us and gave us room to do our jobs. In return, we gave them our very best efforts and loyalty."

What I love about this quote, and I've heard Glynn say it many times, is that it's from his view as an employee or subordinate. He's speaking of the leaders he worked for at NASA—not himself as a leader. For him, the scales of reciprocity were balanced. I have also interviewed people who worked for or with Glynn. They described a very similar balance.

Leadership Insight

In addition to maintaining the balance between leaders and team members, there are the issues of internal and external equity. Internal equity is the comparison of positions within your business to ensure fair pay and treatment. Employees want to perceive that they are paid fairly compared to their coworkers. External equity exists when employees in an organization perceive that they are being rewarded fairly in relation to those who perform similar jobs in other organizations or companies. Human resource experts typically look at an organization's pay rates compared to the average rates in the industries' market or sector to assess external equity.

Again, NASA gives us a different view of equity. NASA boasts the highest employee satisfaction scores of any federal agency and remains the most innovative place in government, according to an annual survey of the best places to work in the federal government.[47]

NASA scored above every other large federal agency in employee satisfaction—which factor in workers' opinions on leadership, pay, work-life balance, and strategic management. The agency also topped the private sector average by more than three points.

Most NASA professionals could make more money in the private sector, but they don't leave because of the work and the leadership.

Tailoring Relationships to Individual Employees

Pay is important. However, research shows that it is rarely the deciding factor in whether employees choose to stay or leave a position. Other factors are much more important. But each employee is different, and their priorities and preferences are different. To connect with them, the best managers inquire about those preferences and then frame their relationship keeping those preferences in mind.

Some questions that can be used to structure a professional relationship include:

- **How would you like to be recognized publicly?** Would you prefer a plaque, for example, or a shout-out at an internal meeting? Do you want your immediate team members to hear the praise about you or is it more important to you that higher-ups are made aware of your skills? Find out what's important to each employee with respect to how your appreciation is communicated.

- **How would you prefer to be rewarded?** Some employees may want a monetary bonus for exceptional performance while others may want a day off in exchange for working over a weekend. For some, more frequent performance reviews would be appreciated. Others may want mentoring, reimbursement for college or graduate level courses, or the opportunity to work from home once a week. By asking, you tailor rewards and make the employee feel truly loved for their contributions.

- **How do you prefer to communicate?** Some employees love receiving phone calls, while others hate it and would much rather have you send them an email. And then there are those employees who swear by text messaging or in-person chats by their cubicle. Learn how they want you to communicate with them and your odds of having your message received and responded to quickly will skyrocket.

- **How can I serve you?** The best leaders inquire about what employees need most to function at their best. By asking this type of question, they're likely to earn the appreciation and loyalty of employees who could really use some support. Such a question might reveal that a new parent could really use a babysitter so that he and his wife can have a night out. Another employee might not want to admit it, but they could really use a tutor to help them get through college level calculus in night school. Another might benefit from being able to work four long days each week so that she can travel out of town to care for her ailing parent.

- **How can I support your career?** Finding out how you can help an employee pursue their career goals is another way to develop a close relationship with them. Asking that question may reveal that one employee is looking for a career mentor. Another may want the chance to lead a highly visible project, or a professional recommendation for an opening in another business unit.

These efforts rarely cost much but can be the difference between retaining a high performer and having them look for greener pastures.

Managers Make the Difference

More important than pay or stock options or vacation days is the social connections people make at work. The friendships forged dramatically increase the likelihood that an employee will remain with an organization long-term.

Gallup[48] research reported that "for men and women, having a best friend at work leads to better performance." The reason for this superior performance, relative to less engaged employees, says Gallup, is that "When employees possess a deep sense of affiliation with their team members, they are driven to take positive actions that benefit the business—actions they may not otherwise even consider if they did not have strong relationships with their coworkers."

Perhaps more important than co-workers, however, is an employee's relationship with his or her manager.

Gallup found, in its "State of the American Manager"[49] report, that managers account for seventy percent of the variance between engaged and disengaged employees. In the US, an estimated thirty-five percent of the workforce is engaged; sixty-five percent are not.

Of course, reciprocity works negatively, too, and relationships can decline into a negative reciprocity spiral, where individuals take turns in passively punishing the other person. For example, an employee who is upset that their manager didn't recommend them for a promotion may decide to work fewer hours, since their contributions aren't appreciated. By cutting back on their hours, their manager may perceive that they've disengaged and aren't interested in the work, leading to fewer opportunities to take on new projects. With fewer new projects, the work becomes boring. Ultimately, the employee is likely to quit or be fired.

The trick to pulling out of a negative reciprocity spiral is to ask questions and gather information about how an employee is feeling about their work, what would make the situation or the environment even better for them, and then taking action. Looking for ways to be of service will enhance professional relationships and lead to employees who couldn't imagine working anywhere else, for anyone else.

It's managers—great managers—that frequently make the difference between poor and good performance, or good and great performance, says Gallup:[50] "Great managers consistently engage their teams to achieve outstanding performance. They create environments where employees take responsibility for their own—and their team's—engagement and build workplaces that are engines of productivity and profitability."

One tactic Lunney used regularly to improve his team's performance and help them bond was the debriefing after each mission. There was the official debriefing held at work behind closed doors where evaluations of what went right and what went wrong were shared. And there was the much more important unofficial debriefing, which was held at the Hofbrau Garden in Dickinson. This was a tradition started by Chris Kraft and held at the German beer garden, well off-site.

It was during the unofficial debriefing, attended by the astronauts, Lunney's team, and others from NASA, that the truth was really shared. "The only protocol was that there was no protocol." Over multiple beers, engineers shared their true feelings about themselves and others, what they did right and what the failures were. There was plenty of teasing, of admissions of fault, and expressions of frustration and anger over others' decisions. It was a time to release the pressure of the mission that had built up and a chance to speak, no holds barred, about what had *really* just gone down.

The Rest of the Story

Glynn told me that only NASA team members attended these events with one exception. Glynn's brother-in-law was visiting and Glynn invited him to come along. His brother-in-law felt a bit awkward in the presence of the astronauts and rocket scientists. So, he asked if it would be okay if he bought a keg of beer for the gathering. After that evening, Glynn's brother-in-law had a standing invitation to attend mission debriefs at the Hofbrau Garden as an auxiliary member of the team.

When awarded the National Rotary Award for Space Achievement, Lunney's leadership skills were cited as a contributing factor to his success: "As a manager, he inspired his employees to do their best work and offered direction and encouragement to his team when challenges arose."

Leadership Insight

I asked Glynn Lunney to review this chapter. To be honest, I was a little hesitant asking one of the pioneers of manned space flight to review my work. After reading the chapter he wrote that he wanted to talk by phone. I was concerned. The first thing he said was that I gave him "far too much credit." He pointed out that many of the leadership approaches that he was known for, he learned from Chris Kraft, Bob Gilruth, and others.

As he spoke, I thought of Jim Collins' book *Good to Great*. His researchers found two distinct characteristics among the best leaders of great companies: humility and a steely determination to do the right thing. A rigorous study by Ou, Waldman & Peterson published in the *Journal of Management* "Do Humble CEOs Matter?" found that humility affects all aspects of business success from pay disparity to financial performance.[51]

I guess it also affects whether you can fly to the moon.

Leadership Experience

To help you apply what you've learned here about the scales of reciprocity and Glynn Lunney's work at NASA, consider these questions:

- How well do you know your team and individual members?

- How do they prefer to feel cared for by you; recognition, time, attention, or something else? Are you sure?

- Do you try to demonstrate to them that you care?

- Are you there for them in tough times—when they have personal or professional difficulties?

- What do you need from your teammates? Have you articulated that to them?

CHAPTER 8

APOLLO 1 — LEADERSHIP IN A CRISIS

"The message to the team is to remember how difficult our business is, the importance of staying focused and using our imaginations to envision what can go wrong."

—William H. Gerstenmaier,
NASA's associate administrator

Unlike previous chapters about Apollo managers as leadership role models, this chapter is about a crisis situation that required skilled leadership. Many leaders—not just one—made it possible for NASA to survive a tragedy and move past it.

With mounting pressure from the Russians to successfully send a man into space, the focus of the US space program in 1958 was on putting one person into space and bringing him back safely. That was the Mercury program. Mercury ran from 1958 until 1963 and consisted of six manned flights, the first of which sent Alan Shepard into space and back again.

Each flight, each program, built on the experiences from the last one. The processes were iterative.

The Mercury program begat the Gemini program—putting two people into space. With Gemini we learned to rendezvous (connecting two spacecraft together in space), tested how astronauts performed during longer space missions, and learned how to move outside a spacecraft on orbit and do spacewalks, all in preparation for the ultimate mission to the moon. While many issues cropped up during these ten manned flights, some having to do with the astronauts and others that were technical in nature, NASA deemed the missions successful. The astronauts always returned to Earth unharmed.

The End of a "Lucky Streak"

The Apollo program followed Gemini. Apollo would place three people into space and eventually land on the moon.

There is an adage that, "It's better to be lucky than good. It's best to be both." Looking back on the successes of Mercury and Gemini, they both had a lot to

Apollo 1 crew training about the NASA Motor Vessel Retriever
in the Gulf of Mexico. From the left: Ed White, Gus Grissom,
and Roger Chaffee. Photo NASA S66-58501

do with luck. And NASA's luck was about to run out, exposing problems that should have—could have—been caught earlier.

On Friday, January 27, 1967, three astronauts were scheduled to conduct a routine preflight launch rehearsal. The space capsule wouldn't leave the ground during the AS-204 "plugs out" test. Instead they would practice what a launch would be like. The crew were in their space suites in the closed-up Command Module when: "We've got a fire." That message came through Grissom's open microphone.

A spark from wires within the capsule caused a flash fire. All three astronauts died of asphyxiation due to inhalation of toxic gases in less than thirty seconds.

The tragedy shook NASA to its core. Everyone knew the dangers of space flight, but this was just a ground test. How could things in the cockpit go so wrong so quickly? How was the program able to make so much progress and then take a monumental step back with the fire?

These were questions the organization began to ask itself.

Looking back, it was obvious the capsule was ripe for a major mishap.

Normalization of the Deviation

Dr. Diane Vaughn, author of *The Challenger Launch Decision*, coined the phrase "normalization of the deviation" to explain the phenomenon that occurs within organizations and groups when they become so accustomed to deviant behavior or results that they no longer consider them unusual. This occurs even when the results exceed agreed-upon rules for safety. The deviance becomes a new normal, a new standard. At NASA, the deviation referred more to level of risk or danger.

With each successive space flight, the agency pushed the acceptable limits farther and farther from what was originally considered safe. People became desensitized to risk. The upper limits of what was considered dangerous were pushed out, until the situation was almost guaranteed to eventually result in a catastrophe.

Unfortunately, no one at NASA recognized the situation until it was too late—the tipping point had been reached.

What was the situation? A few specific factors, technical and organizational, contributed to the deadly event.

Pure oxygen environment. First was the fact that the astronauts were operating in a pressurized pure oxygen environment, which is highly combustible. The Mercury spaceship had originally been designed with an internal atmosphere of pure oxygen instead of mixed gases to save weight.

While that was dangerous, when the missions were successful the fact that the oxygen was flammable seemed to fade into the background. Pure oxygen became the new normal. It became acceptable.

So, of course, the NASA engineers stuck with oxygen for Gemini, despite the fact that weight wasn't as big a factor. They could have switched to mixed gases but didn't because it had been "proven safe"—meaning only that the capsule hadn't exploded. They had become desensitized to the level of danger.

They learned how wrong they were the instant Apollo 1 went up in flames.

Too much wire. There were miles of wire in the Apollo Command Module; inside the cramped spacecraft there were wires everywhere. Wire itself isn't inherently dangerous but in large quantities, where it can be easily bent, stepped on, or have insulation nicked exposing bare wire, the probability of an electrical short increases. With that much wire, the chances of a spark skyrocket.

And that's what happened.

The good news is that following the Apollo 1 disaster, the capsule's interior was redesigned, and wire insulated in a fire-resistant coating that would squelch sparks, even in a pressurized oxygen environment.

Flammable materials. While the cause of the spark was probably a short in a wire near Gus Grissom's legs, the astronauts didn't have enough time to fight the fire or get out because they were enveloped in flammable materials. In particular, the abundance of Velcro proved short-sighted.

Velcro was widely used inside space capsules because the hook-and-loop design made it possible to affix things in a zero-gravity environment. Everything from the astronauts to pens and pencils, reference manuals, and anything else, really, could be attached to Velcro on the walls of the capsule. Unfortunately, because Velcro is highly flammable, its use should have been limited.

Groupthink. Beyond the flaws in the capsule's physical environment was an even bigger indicator of impending disaster—groupthink. Groupthink occurs within teams or organizations when people try to minimize conflict and reach a consensus decision without a critical evaluation of alternative viewpoints. The individuals involved will even choose to ignore red flags or warning signs that pop up along the way. Indicators emerge but the parties involved opt to dismiss, overlook, or ignore them.

NASA engineers and administrators had "willful blindness," a phrase coined by Margaret Heffernan in her book by the same name to refer to intentionally overlooking or looking past warning signs. Red flags appeared with respect to some of the risks being taken on Apollo 1, but people involved turned a blind eye. Rather than speak up about possible issues, they opted to stay silent.

This type of behavior is the definition of groupthink, which psychologist Irving Janis identified as striving to achieve or maintain consensus within a group. Getting to consensus becomes the top priority within the group—more important than voicing concerns or disagreement.

Janis identified eight characteristics or symptoms of groupthink:

1. **Illusions of invulnerability.** This phenomenon causes group members to be overly optimistic, which often leads to high risk behavior. They are unrealistic and assume that failure is nearly impossible.

2. **Unquestioned beliefs.** Rather than exploring potential moral conflicts or the consequences of various actions, group members go with the flow and stay quiet.

3. **Rationalizing.** Rather than consider the possibility of failure, group members push aside warning signs. They concoct stories to reassure themselves that success is inevitable.

4. **Stereotyping.** Anyone who dares question the group's plan or suggests alternatives runs the risk of being ignored or outcast in the name of consensus maintenance.

5. **Self-censorship.** Members of the group who do have doubts decide to bury them rather than voice their concerns.

6. **"Mindguards."** Some members of the group appoint themselves censors and cover up or eliminate information that emerges that is counter to the group's desired outcome. Reports of problems or risks never see the light of day thanks to these guards.

7. **Illusions of unanimity.** Rarely are all members of the group in agreement and aligned, but in groupthink participants convince themselves of this.

8. **Direct pressure to conform.** Members who dare to ask questions, propose other

approaches, or generally appear not in alignment with the group are positioned as disloyal.

Groupthink certainly contributed to the Apollo 1 tragedy. The event brought the march of progress of the manned space program to an abrupt halt. Members of the media and a few politicians, including Senator Walter Mondale, called for an end to the Apollo "moon-doggle." The fire would at least suspend work for a good two years.

Experts often divide crisis management into two parts. How do you "lead in the moment" as the crisis is happening, and then how do you lead an organization out of crisis over the longer term to a new homeostasis? James Webb and Gene Kranz are good exemplars of how to lead in the middle of chaos.

Get me the president. James Webb was at a reception in Washington, DC, when he received a call telling him of the fire at the Cape. He immediately called President Johnson to notify him of the disaster. Webb knew there would be a Congressional investigation and could have also asked for a third-party investigation, to sidestep any political entanglements. However, to get to the bottom of what happened, Webb took the unusual step of asking to allow NASA to handle the investigation internally, according to its established procedure, promising to be truthful in assessing blame, and to keep the appropriate leaders of Congress informed.

Webb's reasoning was that he wanted to show that NASA had the integrity to scrutinize itself. He also wanted to manage the impact to morale inside NASA, which was still pushing forward to get a man on the moon within the decade. Surprisingly, Johnson, the politician, agreed. Webb quickly created the Apollo 204 Review Board, which was made up of NASA executives, researchers, and academics.

Leadership Insight

While we focus here on how NASA learned from the Apollo 1 fire, there can be a danger in focusing too much on learning from failures such as this. We don't want to fall prey to "superstitious learning"—the assumption that there is more to be gleaned from failed missions than from successful ones. One of NASA's best practices is that they run post-mortems on every mission and every simulation.[52]

The Kranz Dictum

There were other leaders who also stepped up—leaders like Gene Kranz, a successor to Chris Kraft as flight director.

Following the cockpit fire, Kranz held an all-hands meeting in the auditorium of Building 30, in the Johnson Space Center. He brought everyone in Mission

Control together in order to recalibrate their mental and emotional states. This is what he told them:

"Spaceflight will never tolerate carelessness, incapacity, and neglect. Somewhere, somehow, we screwed up. It could have been in design, build, or test. Whatever it was, we should have caught it. We were too gung-ho about the schedule, and we locked out all of the problems we saw each day in our work. Every element of the program was in trouble and so were we. The simulators were not working, Mission Control was behind in virtually every area, and the flight and test procedures changed daily. Nothing we did had any shelf life. Not one of us stood up and said, 'Dammit, stop!' I don't know what Thompson's committee will find as the cause, but I know what I find. We are the cause! We were not ready! We did not do our job. We were rolling the dice, hoping that things would come together by launch day, when in our hearts we knew it would take a miracle. We were pushing the schedule and betting that the Cape would slip before we did.

From this day forward, Flight Control will be known by two words: 'Tough' and 'Competent.' Tough means we are forever accountable for what we do or what we fail to do. We will never again compromise our responsibilities. Every time we walk into Mission Control, we will know what we stand for. Competent means we will never take anything for granted. We will never be found short in our knowledge and in our skills. Mission Control will be perfect. When you leave this meeting today you will go to your office and the first thing you will do there is to write 'Tough' and 'Competent' on your blackboards. It will never be erased. Each day when you enter the room these words will remind you of the price paid by Grissom, White, and Chaffee. These words are the price of admission to the ranks of Mission Control."

In little more than 300 words, which took less than five minutes to deliver, Kranz said all the things a true leader needed to say. Although, at that point, he didn't know the cause of the fire, he did know who was at fault—everyone working on the mission. "We screwed up," he confirmed.

In addition to accepting collective responsibility for the tragedy, Kranz also pointed the way forward. "We will never again compromise our responsibilities," he said. He instructed everyone in Mission Control to write the words "Tough" and "Competent" on their office blackboards as constant reminders of what needed to change for future missions to be successful.

We know they did just that because, even today, so many years later, in offices where blackboards have been replaced with whiteboards, you'll find those two words permanently etched on the walls with the note to "Do not erase!"

Kranz's short speech, referred to thereafter as "the Kranz Dictum," helped shift everyone's focus from the failure to the future. He took responsibility, he established values—toughness and competency—and he influenced the narrative about the event.

This strong stance is in sharp contrast to how other leaders have acted in the face of crisis. Leaders like Tony Hayward of British Petroleum (BP), CEO during the massive Deepwater Horizon oil spill in the Gulf of Mexico, who did the exact opposite of Kranz. During the BP oil spill that started in April 2010, Hayward:

- Tried to pin the blame for the accident on the oil rig's owner, Transocean, saying in an interview, "This was not our accident … This was not our drilling rig … This was Transocean's rig. Their systems. Their people. Their equipment."

- Spoke almost callously about the potential damage to the environment, saying, "The Gulf of Mexico is a very big ocean. The amount of volume of oil and dispersant we are putting into it is tiny in relation to the total water volume."

- Then tried to downplay the repercussions, telling reporters, "I think the environmental impact of this disaster is likely to be very, very modest."

- Attempted to cover up the extent of the damage, reporting that the oil flow was 5,000 gallons a day when video footage BP tried to suppress showed the flow was as much as 19,000 gallons a day. Of course, it was in their best interests to minimize estimates of oil production, since civil penalties start at $4,300 per barrel.

- Denied, denied, denied, when scientific studies indicated clouds of oil were forming under-water, claiming, "The oil is on the surface," he said. "There aren't any plumes."

- Tried to gain sympathy for his personal incon-venience, commenting, "I'm sorry. We're sor-ry for the massive disruption it's caused their lives. There's no one who wants this over more than I do. I'd like my life back."

For all of these reasons and more, Hayward was let go in June 2010, following questioning by Congress during which he "couldn't recall" many of the decisions that led to the largest oil spill disaster in US history.

A Willingness to Speak Truth to Power

While Kranz was rallying the troops in Mission Control, another man, George Low, stepped up. Low was the deputy director of the Manned Spacecraft Center in Houston (now named the Johnson Space Center) and one of the chief strategists of NASA's whole human spaceflight program from the formation of the agency in 1958. He made it his personal mission to discover what had gone wrong. Low took a demotion to be the Apollo Spacecraft Program Manager in order to be able to take over responsibility for redesigning the Apollo spacecraft. He would lead the effort in the second stage of crisis management—pulling the organization out of crisis over the longer term to a "new normal."

Low was the ideal candidate for this role for a number of reasons. Most important, he was widely respected as a leader as well as having a reputation for being a talented engineer. He was equally at home in research work or solving practical yet complex technical problems. His boss, Dr. Robert Gilruth, noted, "George was good at everything!" He was known for his integrity, had an amazing work ethic (eighteen-hour workdays were not uncommon for him), and for his willingness to question conventional wisdom. He was comfortable telling his superiors when they were wrong, which was an essential trait as the entire Apollo program was put under a microscope. They couldn't afford to be so wrong again.

He was also tough on people in his search for the technical truth.

Almost immediately, Low set a fast pace. He began a grueling schedule of meetings with engineers and contractors to determine what went wrong and what needed to be changed to avoid future disasters. He would typically leave Houston on Sunday evening. First stop—North American headquarters for a seven a.m. Monday meeting about their findings and proposed solutions. Then back on the airplane flying to contractors across the country to check on different aspects of the capsule design and manufacture. He would return to Houston to meet on Fridays with a newly chartered Change Control Board (CCB). Low insisted that this board would be attended by all the principal players only, no substitutes permitted. There they discussed the progress made, reviewed unresolved issues that had arisen, and made all necessary decisions. The attendees used a different label for those meetings—they were called "The Hell Meetings" because Low pushed them to test each other's thinking. He insisted that everyone ask the tough questions.

Early in his tenure, Low reportedly said that his redesign work was not focused on the fire but on designing a safer spacecraft. He quickly expanded the scope of his work from the cockpit to the entire capsule. Ultimately, he initiated more than 400 major design changes, only forty of which had anything to do with the cause of the fire.

He led people back to a new normal, away from the high-risk, unrealistic normal that had evolved following the successes of Mercury and Gemini.

It's about people. George Low humanized the work, bringing it down from making a safe spacecraft to keeping individual astronauts, who were their friends, alive. One way he did that was by designing a special pin that astronauts were given to hand out to a hard-working employee at each subcontractor they visited. Shaking hands and mixing with vendors became a new role for astronauts as part of Low's plan to help workers understand that the lives of each astronaut, whom they had personally met, were dependent on their good work.

At about the same time, Snoopy creator Charles Schulz had been asked for permission to use Snoopy as a symbol of excellence, which Schulz readily gave. NASA then had sterling silver lapel pins made with Snoopy's likeness in a space suit for the astronauts to award as astronauts made site visits. This fit well with Low's goal of encouraging astronauts to get out and mix and mingle with contractors inside factories, to forge connections with the people whose work would determine if they lived or died. It became a very big deal when an astronaut appeared at your work site and presented an individual worker with a Silver Snoopy. It was often done as a surprise with family members invited to be part of the recognition. Snoopy pins are still given out today and are an extremely rare and valued form of recognition.

The Rest of the Story

Cartoonist Charles "Sparky" Schulz was an avid supporter of the US space program. He welcomed the idea of using Snoopy for the award. Schulz convinced United Feature Syndicate (the distributor of the Peanuts comic strip) to let NASA use "Snoopy the Astronaut" at no cost. Schulz drew a special image to be made into the pin and promotional art that could be used to publicize the award program.[53]

The Apollo 10 mission launched on May 18, 1969. It was a dress rehearsal for the Apollo 11 lunar landing later that year.

May 18, 1969, Snoopy and Charlie Brown sit on top of a
console in the Mission Control Center, Building 30, on the first
day of the Apollo 10 mission. The call sign for the Command
Module was "Charlie Brown." While approaching the moon,
the lunar module's call sign was "Snoopy."
Photo NASA S69-34314

Crises occur in every workplace regularly—while the severity ranges widely, the frequency of occurrence is fairly common. And it's the true leader who knows how to help resolve the problem, such as by redesigning the capsule, and get everyone focused on the way forward, as George Low so skillfully did.

Leadership Experience

The best time to prepare to lead in a crisis is before a crisis breaks out. So how can you prepare to lead? How can you ensure you will be ready to act when needed? Some steps you can think through in advance include:

- Know your derailers. Under stress your worst characteristics may come out. If you know your weaknesses, you can work to keep them in check. The Hogan Personality Inventory is one of the best for this type of personal insight.[54]

- Remaining calm. Margaret Meade said, "Courage is staying calm three seconds longer than everyone else." We've studied this and have some ideas to help you prepare.[55]

- Keeping an eye out for ways you can practice leading during stress in your daily life. Look for ways you can help others experiencing stress.[56]

- Inventorying your skills. What training have you had that might prove useful in a crisis? Have you had CPR training? Do you know how to change a flat tire? What are you able to do?

- Stepping up in big and small ways. Leaders are those people turn to when they don't know how to handle a situation. Think about how you would act, to prepare yourself for the opportunity to make a difference in a crisis.

CHAPTER 9

GEORGE LOW — RISK AND REWARD

"As usual with any great endeavor, it always boils down to a single human being who makes a difference. In the case of Apollo, the person in my mind who made the difference was George Low."

—Apollo 8 commander, Frank Borman

Time to move. Following the fire in the Apollo 1 capsule, George Low took over the capsule redesign. Easy? Not by a long shot. The fire delayed the carefully planned schedule by anywhere between twenty-two to twenty-four months, depending on the source.

President Kennedy's goal of getting a man on the moon by the end of the decade was becoming less and less likely, especially given that during the redesign process, there would be no launches; there was no space travel for two whole years. Doubt was creeping in.

While NASA delayed, the Soviet Union seemed to be systematically moving ahead. By the time of the Apollo 1 fire the Russians had already conducted the first extra-vehicular activity (EVA) or spacewalk, and had made a soft landing on the surface of the moon with the Luna 9 spacecraft. Luna 10 in 1966 was the first probe to successfully achieved a lunar orbit. They also rendezvoused and docked two unmanned spacecraft Cosmos 186 and Cosmos 188.

When NASA suspended launches to investigate the Apollo 1 accident, the Russians achieved a huge milestone. Their Zond 5 spacecraft, carrying live turtles and cultures of human cells, landed on the moon and returned to a landing in the Indian Ocean. The Russians were in the lead. The United States tracked the flight, monitored the communications, and even took photographs of the descent capsule bobbing in the sea. We confirmed that the Russians had put living beings on the moon and brought them home safely.

These deliberate and progressive steps reminded NASA management of the similar course of actions the Soviets had taken to make Yuri Gagarin the first human in space. They started with unmanned probes and tests, then advanced to live animals. It was natural for the Americans to assume cosmonauts would be next.

Leadership Insight

Confirmation bias is the human tendency to search for, favor, and use information that confirms one's pre-existing views on a certain topic. We want to reinforce what we already believe. This is dangerous for leaders because it can lead to flawed decision-making. Imagine the CEO of a company has an idea for a new product or service. She tells marketing to conduct research to explore whether her idea has merit or not. The team conducts focus groups and surveys to see if the boss is right. You can imagine the most probable outcome (of course she is).

NASA management, encouraged by the CIA, fell into the confirmation bias trap. They looked for data that supported their fear that the Soviets were beating us to the moon. In fact, we now know that the Russians had given up on beating us to the moon by 1967.

How can leaders avoid confirmation bias? First, we need to be aware of our own assumptions and biases. Remember your statistics classes—the question you ask or the method of measurement can affect your results. Edward de Bono's famous "Six Thinking Hats" gives us six distinct directions in which our thinking can be challenged. These six directions are easy to use because they are based on our natural ways of thinking.[57] Another way to combat bias is to seek diverse or even contrarian opinions.

How Can we Beat these Guys?

From March 1967 through the summer of 1968, George Low's plan for the redesign of the Apollo Command Module was working. The Change Control Board met in the "hell meetings" ninety times, considered 1,697 changes, and approved 1,341. Alan Shepard wrote, "We were gaining confidence all the while that, yes, they're creating something that will be safe for us to fly."[58]

Low felt good about the progress at NASA. But he also saw the CIA reports on the Soviet progress. In August 1968, George Low went on vacation. Without the day-to-day pressures he looked at the big picture—which of the three rocket components were still on schedule and which were behind. In fact, two of the three elements—the Service Module and the Command Module, were still on target for delivery. It was the lunar lander that was behind schedule and always had been. The next flights, Apollo 7 and 8 were planned to orbit Earth and to test the new systems and module. Apollo 8 would be the first manned flight of the giant Saturn V rocket and test docking with the lunar module. But the lander wasn't ready to test.

What if? Low thought "What if—we went to the moon, but didn't land on it?" NASA could still achieve its goal of being the first humans to the moon. By orbiting the moon and returning, the US could achieve its objective and not have to wait for the lunar lander.

If the rocket wasn't landing, there was no need to continue the pressure on Grumman Aircraft to hurry the development of the lunar lander.

When George Low came back from vacation, he began socializing the idea with key executives.

"We were all taken aback," [Chris Kraft] recalled, when Low proposed the idea for real in August 1968. "It was the boldest decision of the space program," Kraft said.

For Low, it was simply a matter of asking the right question: How can we advance the program with hardware that is ready now? "Navigation to the moon, getting into lunar orbit, the burning of the big engine, the computer programs that were needed for that—we could get all of that out of the way."

By working to get American astronauts to the moon, NASA could still make great progress. Orbiting it would allow NASA to test whether it was possible to travel that far, as well as learn more about the moon, including taking photographs of possible landing sites.

Everyone was feeling the competitive pressure. Low's idea was a shortcut to achieving the vision of the martyred president. The US would be the first to get to the moon, even if no one landed on it.

Leadership Insight

A powerful role of leadership is "framer." Changing the question. Directing the team's attention from *here* to *over there*. Saying "what problem are we really trying to solve?" This requires both a foresight and a courage to look where the team isn't looking and then challenge what they are seeing. George Low changed the question from "How can we speed up the sequence of missions already planned?" to "What if we went to the moon, but didn't land on it?" That's a very different question. It required new ways of thinking. Framing is a powerful leadership tool.

"Too Risky"

To test the waters, Low flew down to meet with Wernher von Braun in Huntsville, Alabama. Von Braun's opinion mattered. Von Braun was wholeheartedly in support.

James Webb, the NASA administrator, however, thought it was too risky.

So Low brought together key executives for a vote. "We need to decide if we're going to the moon," he told them. "We'll go around the table and record everyone's answers." There could be no hesitation or backsliding. No one could later claim to have voted differently.

There were twelve people seated at the table. All seemed to be of like mind. A sampling of some of their recorded responses are below. Notice the tone of their answers to Low's question.

Slayton, Astronaut — *"Only chance to get to the moon before the end of 1969."*

Debus, Cape Launch — *"I have no technical reservations, and I have hope."*

Bowman, Technical Support — *"A shot in the arm for manned space flight."*

Richard, Marshal Flight Ctr. — *"Our lunar capability will be enhanced by flying this mission."*

Schneider, Research Dir. — *"You have my wholehearted endorsement."*

Gilruth, Manned Space Flight Center — *"There is always risk, but this is in path of less risk. In fact, the minimum risk of all Apollo plans."*

Kraft, Flight Director — *"It will not be easy to do, but I have confidence. It should be lunar orbit and not circumlunar."*

Gerald T. Smiley (General Electric) — *"Morale is now high; less than lunar orbit would impact this morale."*

While their eloquent answers are all supportive of the decision to focus on orbiting the moon, the language used and the sentiment expressed is rather unusual for men considered the tech giants of NASA. Notice the words they used. Rather than focusing on logic and the risk involved, almost every response is emotion-based. Words and phrases such as "hope," "our only chance," and "a shot in the arm" reflect the men's feelings. They disclose how the men truly felt.

They were emotional sentiments.

We may think we're rational thinkers. Decision-making can be highly emotional even when it appears otherwise. This is the human side of risk assessment, which leads to an emotional response.

Leadership Insight

One cause of our emotional response to risk and decision-making is a biological response called the amygdala hijack. Joseph LeDoux identified that the amygdala or emotional part of our brains react to any stimulus or new information slightly ahead (in milliseconds) of the frontal cortex or rational part of our brain.

Those milliseconds can be critical. They trigger the fight, flight, or freeze response to handle danger. However, they can also cause us to jump quickly to the wrong conclusion or decision. This emotional reaction can be positive as well as negative. When we giggle impulsively at a joke or event, that's our amygdala reacting. As a leader you need to control your emotional reactions and your mind. Experts believe leaders can do this. "Once your emotional system learns something, it seems you never let it go. What therapy does is teach you how to control it—it teaches your neocortex how to inhibit your amygdala. The propensity to act is suppressed, while your basic emotion about it remains in a subdued form."[59] Followers need leaders who are in control of themselves.

We think of decision-making as almost mathematical in its rationality. We think of the probability of something happening and the magnitude of the outcome (either good or bad). If I drive over the speed limit, what's the probability that a policeman will catch me and what is the price of a ticket? It's all very logical.

Let's take another common example, the act of buying a lottery ticket. Millions of people buy tickets. You've probably bought one. Why? Granted, the cost, or risk, is low, since tickets only cost a dollar or two. There is little downside and a huge upside if you win. The magnitude of a win, or the impact, is extremely high when millions and even hundreds of millions of dollars are at stake. The odds of winning the most recent Powerball as I write this is 1 in 302,575,350. But the probability is virtually zero. According to *The Economist* magazine, the odds of being killed by an asteroid impact are 1 in 74,817,414 or four times greater than winning the lottery. So, why do you and so many other people buy their tickets—because of hope. That's just the word Kurt Debus used in his response to George Low. It's the emotional part of the brain overriding the rational brain.

The Rest of the Story

The lack of diversity among the key Apollo 8 decision-makers may have affected the team's perception of risk—I'll call it "the white male effect." All of the major players were white males. Researchers have found that sex and race have a strong effect on risk perception.

According to Paul Slovic, "This effect is so pronounced that it is found in almost every study of risk perception, and it is still unclear how it comes about. Men are different. Generally, males perceive risks to be smaller than females do. White males perceived risks to be less than black males."[60] This is not necessarily biological, as most of this research has been done in North America and Europe. Culture affects perception. But it does imply that more diversity in groups making decisions should be able to mitigate unseen biases such as the white male effect.

Back to the decision to fly Apollo 8 to the moon and the statements by the NASA executives. The risks were great. The odds of another explosion or problem was high, despite the months of redesign work invested in the Command Module. The Saturn V rocket had never been used with a manned fight. They couldn't take the lunar lander along to serve as a lifeboat. The plan had always been, that in case you have an engine problem on the command ship, that you have a whole other spacecraft there to get you out of trouble. You could use its engine to get home. In fact, that's what did happen on Apollo 13. But on Apollo 8—no Plan B. The risks were high.

Looking back, we should look at not only what the answers were to the question of going to the moon early, but how was the question asked?

Astronaut Frank Borman remembered Deke Slayton calling him into his office and telling him, "Look, the CIA has got hard evidence that the Soviets are going to try a manned circumlunar flight before the end of the year. Your lunar module has slipped. It isn't going to be ready until February at the earliest. Can you get ready—this was August—and change the Apollo 8 flight and go to the moon?"[61]

The question was not "should we go?"

The risk was high and the perceived payoff, or magnitude, is also high. The impact of a successful flight would be huge for the space program. Likewise, another failure could be catastrophic for NASA, and the country's reputation as a whole. There was a lot on the line.

We now look back at Apollo 8 with confident hindsight. If the flight had failed, it would have been very different. I'm not saying whether the decision was right or wrong. However, I do question the way in which the decision was made. Failure to take one more look at whether the criteria for the risk had been met may have been missed. Effective leaders recognize the importance of balancing the emotional and rational self. They understand that there is always an emotional side of decision-making and can take steps to counter it, to try and ensure that the potential reward equals the risk being taken.

Look Out for these Factors

Besides the general danger of our emotions affecting our decision-making, what specific tendencies should we guard against? David Ropeik at the Harvard Medical School has identified the major factors that affect our perception of risk:[62]

Trust. The more we trust the people informing us of risks, the lower we perceive the danger. In the case of Apollo 8, all of the key decision-makers had worked together for many years and respected each other's work.

Origin. People are less concerned about risks they incur themselves than the ones that others impose on them. I'm more fearful of the driver next to me using a cell phone than when I use my phone while driving.

Control. Many more people are afraid of flying than of driving even though we know that statistically, automotive travel is much more dangerous. If we read the narratives of the Apollo 8 decision, we can see that the engineers were most confident of the portions of the flight for which they were responsible.

Nature. Natural dangers, such as the radiation from the sun is perceived as relatively harmless. Man-made radiation such as from nuclear power plants is feared.

Scope. Catastrophic events, such as earthquakes and tsunamis, are scarier than, say, heart disease, which kills many more people. Safety experts will tell you that the primary causes of injuries in the workplace are from trips, falls, and overexertion.

Awareness. Media coverage and hype that raises our awareness of particular risks can create a disproportionate fear. Think of the television show *Shark Week* that comes on every summer.

Risk vs. benefit. The more we perceive a benefit from a dangerous act the less fearful we are of the risk. We see this in recreational activities such as bungee jumping or even drug use. The teams at NASA saw Apollo 8 as having scientific, national, and morale benefits.

The Rest of the Story

One factor that may have affected the decision to take Apollo 8 to the moon was the sense of inevitability. In Kennedy's famous Rice speech, he asked rhetorically,

"Why, thirty-five years ago, fly the Atlantic?" referring to Charles Lindbergh's flight from New York to Paris.

The night before the launch of Apollo 8, Charles Lindbergh and his wife, Anne Morrow Lindbergh, visited the crew at their quarters in the Kennedy Space Center. They talked about how, before his 1927 flight, Lindbergh had used a piece of string to measure the distance from New York City to Paris on a globe and, from that, calculated the fuel needed for the flight. The total he had carried was a tenth of the amount that the Saturn V would burn every second. The next day, the Lindberghs watched the launch of Apollo 8 from a nearby dune.

A Salve for the Nation

As it turns out, all the work redesigning the capsule paid off. There was no fire, no catastrophic event, and all three astronauts returned home safely after their trip around the moon. Apollo 8 was a huge success and helped propel the space program forward.

It was an important event in and of itself, but even more so because of the awful events that occurred in 1968. The list is lengthy and includes, but is not limited to:

- Robert Kennedy being killed.

- Martin Luther King, Jr. being assassinated.

- A country divided over the Vietnam War.

- Race riots in many northern cities including Washington, Chicago, and Baltimore.

- Protesters being beaten at the Democratic Convention.

Apollo 8 saved 1968. Fortunately, the year ended with the three astronauts reading from the Bible. On Christmas Eve they recorded a reading from the Book of Genesis, about God creating the heaven and Earth, and sent it back to Earth. Soon thereafter the astronauts themselves returned to Earth, proving that the US could safely send men into space.

The first time humans saw an Earth rise. Taken by William
Anders on December 24, 1968, at 10:40 a.m. Houston time.
The South Pole is to the left, North and South America partially
covered in clouds. Photo NASA as08-14-2383

Leadership Experience

Everyone assesses risk and reward differently. As a leader,
it's useful to know how you approach decision-making.

To learn how you approach risk and reward, ask
yourself some questions:

- How does my personality, values, and ambi-
  tion affect my decisions?

- How can I balance my emotions against rationality in assessing risk?

- How often do we seek diverse opinions or ask, "What's wrong with my plan?" to others with differing opinions?

- How can I guard against the biases identified by Harvard Medical School?

CHAPTER 10
APOLLO 13—
RESPONSIVE INNOVATION

"Adaptability and constant innovation are the
keys to the survival of any company operating
in a competitive market."

—Shiv Nadar

The world watched for seven days as astronauts Jim
Lovell, Jack Swigert, and Fred Haise battled their way
back to Earth following a mission-crippling explosion
on board the Apollo 13 spacecraft. The mission started
smoothly enough with a liftoff of the giant Saturn V
rocket from Cape Canaveral, Fla., on April 11, 1970,

and sent the crew on their way to the moon for an expected third lunar landing for the NASA team.

The spaceship itself was composed of two key pieces. The Command Module, call sign Odyssey, was the mother ship. It would orbit the moon with one crewman while the second piece, the lunar module, would fly down to the moon. Its call sign was Aquarius. Two days from launch and 200,000 miles from Earth, Mission Control noticed a low-pressure warning signal on one of the hydrogen tanks on Odyssey. Then there were some unusual fluctuations in one of the oxygen tanks. Thinking that the signals might be corrected by mixing the cryogenic liquids/gases in the tanks to make them operate more efficiently, Mission Control called for a "cryo stir" (activating heaters inside the tanks). Swigert was instructed to flip a switch to perform the routine mixing.

However, instead of routinely mixing the hydrogen and oxygen within the tanks, the cryo stir caused an explosion. That killed the power within the ship and depleted the oxygen. The entire spacecraft shook and Lovell alerted Mission Control, "Houston, we've had a problem."

That event kicked off four successive days of problem-solving, trouble-shooting, and praying for a miracle that would bring the ship and its passengers back safely to Earth. With power gone in the Command Module, the astronauts relocated to Aquarius. But the lunar module was designed only to take two astronauts to the lunar surface and support them for a couple of days. The three astronauts survived in that little space until it was time to re-enter the Earth's atmosphere in the Odyssey Command Module.

It was later discovered that a design error left wires exposed in an oxygen tank and when one sparked during the cryo stir, it set off a chain reaction causing an explosion and significant damage to the ship.

The dramatic story of the crisis on board Apollo 13 has been used by many people from Paul Hersey and Ken Blanchard to *Forbes* magazine to illustrate a number of leadership lessons. The leadership take-aways that emerged from the mission are varied and important, but we're going to focus on just two aspects: responsive innovation and short-term visioning.

The Rest of the Story

Anyone who has watched the movie *Apollo 13*, which Ron Howard directed and Tom Hanks starred in, may wonder how accurate it was. Most movies embellish details or introduce new situations for dramatic effect. Not so much this one. *Apollo 13* is a highly accurate portrayal of the events surrounding the events that occurred on board the spaceship.

Engineers at NASA circulated a paper entitled, "The 17 Things Wrong with the Movie *Apollo 13*." For example: The rocket plume flaring from the Saturn V as it ascends after liftoff is too small and too short. The plume would be at least twice the diameter of the entire craft and at least three times the length. The other errors are equally minor. Enjoy the film. It's right on!

Innovating Responsively

Many organizations today are working toward being more innovative. Many CEOs have stated their intent to invest in innovation as a path to greater financial success. But some seem to have confused creativity with innovation—they're not synonymous.

The main difference between creativity and innovation is focus. Creativity, at its most basic form, is generating new, different, and revolutionary ideas or solutions. It's making something new out of nothing. Creative ideas are like experiments of the mind. Creativity is hard to measure.

Innovation is measurable. Innovation is about introducing change into and already existing system or process. Innovation typically requires effort to make the idea usable or feasible.[63]

I've seen many companies pursue creativity when they want practical innovation. The editor of the *Harvard Business Review*, Theodore Levitt said: "What is often lacking is not creativity in the idea-creating sense but innovation in the action-producing sense, i.e. putting ideas to work."[64] Companies such as Apple and Tesla illustrate innovation. The ideas coming out of those companies while radical are also practical.

In the case of Apollo 13, creativity would not have helped. They needed to innovate. But the innovation wasn't just for improvement, it was in response to a series of very specific problems—responsive innovation.

Responsive innovation is finding a new and different way to address a situation that has emerged. In the case of Apollo 13, it was innovation on the fly. It is reactive, yet practical, unlike pure creativity. As parameters change, new ideas are developed.

The Rest of the Story

One area where the movie isn't entirely accurate is in its focus on Gene Kranz as the flight director throughout the entire incident. The accident occurred during a shift change in Mission Control. Gene Kranz and his team were ending their shift and Glynn Lunney's team was coming in. Lunney worked the first twelve-hour shift and dealt with the biggest shocks and surprises of the mission. Gene's team went to the back rooms to problem-solve specific issues. And there were two other flight directors and teams working various shifts throughout the crisis: Milt Windler and Gerry Griffin. Anyone who has met Gene Kranz knows he's a colorful character, and Ed Harris made his character come alive in the film.

With responsive innovation, you're working within boundaries—factors that limit potential solutions. Working with Coca-Cola I learned a concept—"Freedom within a framework," meaning that ideas are always welcome as long as they stay within particular boundaries. Those boundaries could include, among other things, time, cost, ethics, and the law.

During Apollo 13's voyage, there was an ongoing need for responsive innovation, for brainstorming within the parameters of what the astronauts had to work with. They couldn't get supplies from anywhere else, so solutions had to make use *only* of what was on the spaceship.

That was Ken Mattingly's challenge when asked to get more amperage to Odyssey by replicating the problems in a simulator. In his quest to do that, he told those around him to limit his resources to whatever the astronauts had in their ship. When they offered him a flashlight to see better, Mattingly told those around him, "Don't give me anything they don't have." He set boundaries for his innovating that would allow him to find more practical solutions. He could focus on potential answers rather than wasting time developing ideas that would never work.

Too often, companies that want to encourage innovation within their workforce fail to provide boundaries. That hurts more than it helps, actually. Because in most companies, regions, or industries, there are limitations you face that will impact innovation. Pretending they don't exist causes employees to spin their wheels unnecessarily, generating creative ideas that won't ever work, because they ignore the pre-existing boundaries.

Problem-solving is everyone's job, but the leader has a specific role in driving responsive innovation.

First the leader has to define the problem. What has changed that is driving us to need a new solution? In Apollo 13, it was a physical accident. In companies, it could be anything that disrupts the current state. We're trying to answer the question why. Why do we need to innovate? The second step is defining the boundaries or the level of freedom. The third job is to paint a picture of the desired end result. What does the vision of success look like?

The Importance of Short-Term Visioning

Can you see the future? All leaders have a vision of their desired outcome or the way they want things to go. It's a picture in their mind of how their actions will lead to a successful result or resolution—an internal movie of the desired conclusion to their current challenge or opportunity.

In the case of Apollo 13, Gene Kranz had a vision of the desired outcome—getting all three astronauts safely back from the moon. Along the way, as more information emerged about their deteriorating situation, that vision was revised and modified to fit the new variables that had been identified. Like when it was discovered that the capsule was about to go off-course on its return flight, instructions were sent to fire the rocket engine to reorient the ship. Or when the power began to fail and Ken Mattingly was assigned the task of figuring out how to take what little power was left and reallocate it to the capsule to allow it to land.

The overarching vision, as Kranz explained, was getting the astronauts back. To make the situation as clear as possible, he drew a simple picture on the blackboard of the challenge and the desired outcome. Two circles; the Earth and the moon. A line showing the path of the spacecraft.

"They're here and we need to get them here," he explained as he drew.

The drawing couldn't have been clearer. Being able to communicate a vision to others is an important leadership skill. Without that ability to share their vision, leaders can't rally the troops or tap into the brainpower and connections that their teammates have. Lacking that skill, they aren't as effective.

Keep it Simple

The quintessential story I've heard about this, outside of NASA, involves former Chrysler CEO Lee Iacocca. Iacocca recognized that Chrysler had to work quickly to turn things around, to generate sales, or the company would go under. So, he did a little research and discovered that there were no US carmakers selling convertibles any more. There was a hole in the market he wanted to try and fill. So, he asked his engineers to come back with a plan for a new Chrysler convertible.

They did, outlining a twenty-seven-month plan—meaning three model years—to design, prototype, and roll out a new convertible.

Iacocca thought that answer was ridiculous. Did they not understand that time was of the essence?! Chrysler didn't have three model years left if they couldn't introduce a new model.

As the story goes, after hearing the twenty-seven-month proposal, Iacocca walked over to the window of the conference room and called the engineers over. "See that blue LeBaron in the parking lot?" he asked them. "Cut off the top."

And with that solution, Iacocca simplified their task: take an existing car model and find a way to remove the top. Voila! You've got a convertible, in a fraction of the time an entirely new design would have taken.

Leadership Insight

IBM was on life support when Lou Gerstner joined the company. Over a few years he turned the company around. In observing his approach, I noticed he seemed to always break issues into three parts. When he proposed a solution, he had three alternatives. When presenting an idea he had three reasons. He once explained, "This is a complex business. Part of our role as leaders is to make the complex simple."

I later learned that "The Rule of Three" is a McKinsey "pro-tip."[65] Lou had been a McKinsey consultant early in his career. It was originally developed as a guide in creating a persuasive argument. But it also works in problem-solving and handling responsibilities.[66]

In the case of Apollo 13, Kranz had to quickly harness the intelligence of everyone in the room and help them shift gears away from the old plan—the old plan of getting the astronauts safely on and off of the moon. For so many months everyone had been focused on getting the three astronauts onto the moon that it would take significant effort to mentally adjust that focus. Only NASA didn't have time for reflection—they had to reorient their thinking and their vision, quickly!

Kranz could see that some engineers were struggling to shift their attention from a moon landing to a rescue mission, which is why he reverted to simple visual stimuli—his blackboard drawing. He had to help them throw away the old plan they had labored over and instead turn their attention to the crisis at-hand. Simple graphics helped make the situation clear.

It's a leader's responsibility to reduce complex topics to easy-to-understand and digest concepts, which is exactly what Kranz did.

He simplified the complex message of figuring out how to get the capsule back to Earth by drawing pictures. In Mission Control, Kranz drew a picture of the spaceship's current trajectory versus their planned course. They would soon be headed off course and not have the power to reorient their path. In his drawing, Kranz included Earth, the moon, and the capsule that needed to be sling-shotted back towards home.

But a visual presentation isn't always required. Leaders can create a picture of a future state by speaking them, as Jim Lovell did onboard Apollo 13 when Fred Haise was ill and suffering from a urinary tract infection, shivering from the cold. To help Haise picture the very near future, Lovell hugged him tight for warmth and reminded him of where they were headed:

> "Just a little while longer, Freddo. Just a little while longer, we're gonna hit that water in the South Pacific. Open up that hatch. It's eighty degrees out there."

I met Fred Haise at Space Center Houston while we were both waiting to speak to groups. I asked him about that scene in the film when Jim Lovell hugged him and painted that mental picture. I asked whether that really happened. He replied that when you're really cold, human warmth can mean a lot. "We just kept putting off the worry as we focused on the next problem and how to solve it."[67]

This spoken imagery is exactly what President John F. Kennedy used when he stated his intention to put a man on the moon within ten years. He articulated his goal, an American on the moon, within a finite time frame, namely by the end of the decade, and made success measurable, determined by whether NASA got an astronaut on the moon or not.

Three very happy men are welcomed by Rear Admiral Donald Davis. From the left, Fred Haise (waving), John Swigert, and James Lovell Jr. aboard the USS *Iwo Jima*.
NASA Photo S70-35606

Leadership Insight

Did Gene Kranz really say, "Failure is not an option?" Well, yes and no. When the scriptwriters of the film *Apollo 13* interviewed Gene Kranz, they asked him if he ever doubted whether the crew would return safely. He responded, "Failure was not an option." They loved the phrase so much that some wanted to use it as the title of the movie. Kranz used it as the title of his book. But he also says he doesn't remember saying those words during the flight.

I've interviewed many who worked in Mission Control during Apollo 13. Sy Liebergot, one of the flight controllers put it best. "I don't recall those exact words, but that was definitely the frame of mind of all of the flight directors. It was said in many ways."

Leading effectively often involves quick decision-making, based on years of past experience and knowledge of established parameters or boundaries. Being able to assess what you have to work with, which factors are most important to consider, and then communicating your current situation simply is critical for success.

Leadership Experience

There is a scene in *Apollo 13* when Gene Kranz faces several engineers who have come to him for help with the issue of rising carbon dioxide. Kranz has to quickly decide which pieces of the problem he will take responsibility for addressing and which he will outsource.

In that moment, he had to assess which work only he could do and then delegate everything else. In choosing to delegate he demands responsive innovation. "Well I suggest you gentlemen figure out how to put a square peg in a round hole rapidly."

This is an important exercise. To figure out, just as Gene Kranz did, which tasks need responsive innovation and how to manage that.

- How can you recognize which problems can be addressed with routine approaches and which need innovation?

- Do you know your team members' strengths well enough to know who is best suited to innovate on a particular issue?

- What boundaries do you place around people to guide their innovation? Do you include those required by law or by your own personal ethics?

- What can you do to foster innovation better than anyone else? (What skills or experience do you have that no one else does?)

CHAPTER 11
APOLLO 15 — ETHICS IN SPACE

"Integrity has no need of rules."

—Albert Camus

One of the biggest ethical issues within the space program came to a head, oddly enough, due to life insurance. Astronauts couldn't get standard life insurance like you or me because insurance companies wouldn't provide it. Insurers didn't want to sell policies to men who were committed to an endeavor as risky as riding a spaceship toward the moon. Pictures of rockets blowing up and the fire on Apollo 1 were convincing that astronauts could be a money-losing proposition.

This left astronauts concerned about providing for their families if something did go wrong on a mission.

When space flight first hit the national consciousness, a couple of insurance companies stepped up and offered to insure NASA astronauts for free in exchange for being able to say they were NASA's official insurance partner (much like companies today pay for the right to claim they are the official vitamin or energy drink of US Olympic athletes).

While that proposal solved the immediate problem of providing life insurance, it created a new dilemma when other companies offered similar deals: a promotional partnership in exchange for free or low-cost goods. A local car dealer, for example, offered a Corvette to the original seven astronauts for $1/year. The astronauts got a great deal on some temporary wheels and the dealer was then able to resell the used car after a year for much more than it was worth, thanks to it having been driven by John Glenn or Alan Shepard or their colleagues.

Seeing that the promotional offers provided a slippery slope to unethical deal-making, NASA clamped down on it, stating in no uncertain terms that no astronauts could accept free products and services. Such an arrangement created a potential conflict of interest and Deke Slayton, who was put in charge of the Astronaut Corps, took his role as ethics watchdog seriously.

Unfortunately, that prohibition against freebies meant astronauts, once again, had only the limited government life insurance as either military personnel in their branch or as civilian NASA employees. They had no way to ensure that their families would be financially whole if an accident occurred.

So, as a group, the astronauts quietly came up with a plan that could generate some cash in the event of an accident.

The Life Insurance "Plan B"

The plan involved something called "covers"—envelopes signed by astronauts and postmarked on important dates. Before launch, the astronauts signed the covers. They would then give them to a friend. And on important days—the day of the launch, the day the astronauts landed on the moon—their friend got the envelopes to the post office to be postmarked. The covers were then distributed to the astronauts' families. It was life insurance in the form of autographs. If they did not return from space, their families could sell them. Some covers have eventually sold for thousands of dollars.

Even more valuable were "flown" covers, which were signed envelopes that astronauts carried with them on their flights. These covers were thin enough and small enough that a few could easily fit into an astronaut's Personal Preference Kit (PPK). As on the Gemini project, the Apollo astronauts were authorized by NASA to carry a small number of personal mementos on their missions in the PPK. These items were packed into the small beta cloth bags which were closed with a drawstring. The standard PPK bags measured roughly 8" x 4" x 2".

Anything placed in the kit had to be approved by NASA, but few items were denied. Many men brought photos of their family or their mom. Others brought pins or knick-knacks to give their friends later. A market quickly developed for these "flown objects." What had started out as a supplement to the meager government life insurance was changing. But then it blossomed into something more on Apollo 15.

The Rest of the Story

Buzz Aldrin brought a mini chalice and container of wine on Apollo 11 so that he could have communion on the moon. Aldrin was also an elder at Webster Presbyterian Church, and before he headed into space, he got special permission to take bread and wine with him to space and give himself communion.

In the pause before he and Armstrong suited up to step outside, he told Houston, "I would like to request a few moments of silence. I would like to invite each person listening in, wherever and whomever he may be, to contemplate for a moment the events of the past few hours and to give thanks in his own individual way." He brought the communion set back with him and donated it to his church.

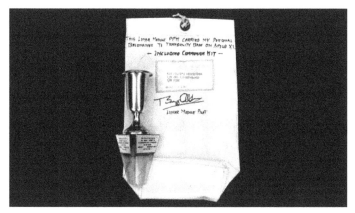

Photo courtesy of David Frohman, President Peachstate
Historical Consulting, Inc.

"A Regular Goddamn Scandal"

What started as a few envelopes contained within a
personal effects kit quickly blossomed beyond that
once the opportunity for profit was recognized. If a
couple of envelopes were worth a few thousand dollars,
imagine what hundreds would be worth, the conversation likely went. So, the three astronauts slated to
fly on Apollo 15, David Scott, Alfred Worden, and
James Irwin, smuggled 400 unauthorized envelopes
onboard. They had arranged in advance to sell 100 of
the envelopes to a German collector for $7,000, and
then they each kept an additional 100 envelopes for
their own use, as an investment of sorts.

If you can picture how much space 400 standard
envelopes take up, you'll recognize that they won't fit in

a small box. Nor can you hide them in your space suit. Getting the envelopes cancelled and then smuggled aboard Apollo 15 took planning and coordination, but they managed to do it successfully. The plot was only discovered on their return, once they were aboard the aircraft carrier and in need of the ship's postmaster's help to cancel them. Turns out, he wasn't so discreet.

The Rest of the Story

In late October 1971, a potential customer for one of the postal covers wrote to NASA about the authenticity of the envelopes. Deke Slayton wrote back saying NASA could not confirm anything about the covers. But the discussion didn't end there. Whether the covers were real became the source of discussion among stamp collectors and sellers. On March 11, 1972, Lester Winick, president of a group of collectors of space stamps and covers known as the Space Topics Study Group, sent a letter to NASA's general counsel asking a series of detailed questions about the Apollo 15 covers. Once the lawyers and media were involved the "cover was blown."

Upon discovery of their plans, Slayton was said to be deeply offended by the astronauts' greed, telling them that they had "violated the public's trust" in trying to make money off their role. From Slayton's perspective, space flight was an act of service, not a business opportunity. "We're doing this for humankind," he told them, "we're not here to make money from it." In his autobiography, Slayton wrote that he confronted Scott and Worden about what he called a "regular goddamn scandal," "they told me what the deal was, and I got pretty goddamn angry. I was through with Scott, Worden, and Irwin. After 16 splashed down, I kicked them off the backup crew for 17."[68]

But Slayton's rebuke was just the start of problems for the astronauts' careers. Their ethical lapse morphed into a legal battle. In early June 1972, George Low learned that unauthorized covers from Apollo 15 were being sold in Europe. Low conferred with associate administrator Dale D. Myers and others. Myers led an internal investigation and made an interim report to Low on the sixteenth. But before he could conclude his inquiry, the story broke with an article in *The Washington Sunday Star*. Low ordered a full investigation by NASA's inspections division. NASA confiscated the envelopes and sent the astronauts back to the military branch from which they had come in disgrace, effectively demoting them. They would never go on another mission.

The astronauts felt that their treatment was somewhat undeserved, pointing out that they were not the first to take envelopes into space. They weren't the ones who had created the market for covers, they argued. Scott admitted that he had made a bad decision, but also felt NASA was turning the whole thing into a "witch-hunt." I've interviewed Al Worden. He also says he made a mistake and that "NASA fired me for it." James Irwin left NASA to become a minister. He has said that the incident helped him in empathizing with others who had erred.

Apollo 15 was an amazingly successful mission. It's the mission that found the "Genesis Rock" formed during the earliest stages of the solar system and tested to be over four billion years old. It's regrettable that in many circles it's best known for the "postal covers scandal."

Hubris Syndrome

How could men of such regard be drawn into a scheme like this? The astronauts had fallen victim to hubris syndrome, which is what happens to some people when they reach the pinnacle of their profession and begin to feel that they are special, or that they don't have to follow the rules that others do, now that their inordinate talents have been recognized.

Some scientists wonder if this syndrome is acquired once an individual reaches the height of their career. That the more they are promoted and rewarded, the more their ego grows, and they become susceptible to the condition.

Those afflicted by hubris syndrome develop a false view of themselves and the world. They begin to see themselves as superior, even untouchable. Many perceive their professional positions as an opportunity to enhance their own wealth and social station—that they are entitled to exploit it as a benefit of that position.

Some become overly concerned with their public image—of how they are perceived. They convince themselves that they can get away with anything. They believe that they are above the law or that rules don't apply to them, because they're special. They begin to see the world as "an arena in which to exercise power and seek glory," report researchers David Owen and Jonathan Davidson in their article in the publication Brain on hubris syndrome in government.[69]

That's exactly what happened to astronauts Scott, Worden, and Irwin. They lost sight of their special role. Instead, they thought of themselves as (rightfully) privileged and looked for ways to exploit it. They likely began to think that the space program was more successful *because* of them and, therefore, that they were entitled to enrich themselves at its expense.

Of course, the astronauts are not the first to fall victim to this syndrome, nor were they the last. Just in the last few years we've seen too many similar situations in business. I admired award-winning journalist and talk show host Charlie Rose for his intellect and interviewing skill. He was fired for sexual misconduct by CBS and PBS. Nissan Motor Company's CEO Carlos Ghosn was fired, not due to misbehavior on the job, but for underreporting his salary on his personal tax returns and other financial missteps, like personal use of corporate assets. The list goes on.

Leadership Insight

I'm not a big fan of the television show *Dr. Phil*. But he has two questions he often asks that I love: "What were you thinking when you did that?" and "How's that working out for you?" When we look at the data sharing by Facebook and Alphabet, the scandals with Bill O'Reilly and 21st Fox, the self-destructive culture at Uber, or diesel-gate at Volkswagen, we have to ask, "What were they thinking?"

We need people to question our actions. In 2016, Shannon Sullivan, a Disney college intern, reported a sign in the employee break room that offended her. A young boy had been killed earlier by an alligator. If asked whether there are alligators, the sign instructing employees to say "'Not that we know of, but if we see one, we will call Pest Management to have them removed.' Please do not say that we have seen them before."[70] Shannon posted a photo of the sign and her outrage on social media. She was fired the next day. Then the issue was brought to the attention of Magic Kingdom Vice President Dan Cockerell. He paid a personal visit to Sullivan and offered her the job back.

Disney showed that, at least in this case, it's okay for someone to question the ethics of a management decision. Disney also gets high marks for its transparency which communicates to others that it's okay to ask difficult questions.

Setting Standards isn't Enough

The truth is, those three astronauts may have been punished so severely in order to send a message to anyone else within NASA who was taking advantage of their position—NASA wasn't having it. Today, astronauts are forbidden by federal regulation from taking philatelic items into space as mementoes.

There were clear standards of behavior for military and government personnel on using their jobs for profit. In addition, Deke Slayton as head of the Astronaut Corps had set the standards even before the Apollo 15 mission and had communicated them within the organization—no taking advantage of your position as astronaut. Despite the stated rules, the three men had done just that—taken advantage of their positions. So, what else can we do to prevent hubris syndrome in leaders?

A 2013 study by Cambridge University sheds some light on possible solutions.[71] The representative sample of Fortune 500 CEOs over a six-year period found that overconfident CEOs tend to make more risky decisions about mergers and acquisitions than more typical CEOs. A dose of humility can be an antidote.

Jim Collins in his book *Good to Great* holds that among the many characteristics that distinguish great companies from others, is that they all had a "Level 5 leader." Level 5 leaders direct their ego away from themselves and toward the success of the organization.

In fact, Collins holds that the first step to becoming a Level 5 Leader is to develop humility. It's the foundational characteristic of the best leaders he studied.

To develop humility in top executives you must instill humility as an organizational value. This can inoculate your whole organization, but particularly those stars who are most vulnerable to hubris. Make humility a virtue. In Shakespeare's *King Lear*, the fool warns the ill-fated monarch, "Have more than thou showest; speak less than thou knowest." This is hard to do today, in our society where personal branding and even grandstanding is commonplace.

Even if you emphasize humility as a value, it won't ensure that one of your "stars" won't try to draw unmerited attention to him or herself for a big success. When that happens, it may be time for some of what Bill Milliken calls "tough love." Milliken emphasizes that the correction is for the long-term interests of the individual as well as the organization. And, most people admire humility and enjoy rooting for humble leaders.

In addition to establishing humility as an organizational value, we should keep a watchful eye for certain behaviors. Without becoming amateur psychologists there are certain individual behaviors exhibited by executives that may reveal developing hubris. Not taking responsibility when things go wrong and blaming others is one. The inverse—taking credit for others' work can also be an indicator. Taking disagreement or feedback as a personal slight is another. The most obvious behaviors are flouting rules because they don't believe the rules apply to them, arrogance, or insisting on behaviors in others that they themselves ignore.

Standards of Perception

Part of the challenge as leader is being aware of how situations may be perceived. Even when you may be doing absolutely nothing wrong—maybe even something good—it's possible an outsider may misread your intentions and call your ethics into question. It's important to be aware of this and take steps to prevent a misunderstanding.

The Rest of the Story

The postal covers were not the only shady deal on Apollo 15. David Scott left a small abstract statue of an astronaut on the moon to honor those who had lost their lives in the pursuit of space exploration. The *Fallen Astronaut* statuette was made by sculptor Paul Van Hoeydonck. Scott claims that Van Hoeydonck promised that he would not make copies. After the flight, the Smithsonian National Air and Space Museum bought a replica for display at the museum. The astronauts acted as intermediaries for the sale. After that transaction, Van Hoeydonck began marketing replicas himself. NASA obviously found out about this commercialization of space memorabilia and protested. Van Hoeydonck stopped selling the statues.

A friend of mine has a teenage daughter who attends a small private school. All the students and teachers know each other well, which is by design. One of the benefits of attending a smaller school is that teachers know students by name, and vice versa.

One day her daughter stayed after school to watch a basketball game and asked her advisor, a thirty-something-year-old man, who had also stayed to watch the game, if she could have a ride home. It was an innocent request and she assured him that there was no pressure, she could call someone else if he didn't have time.

He declined apologetically, not because he didn't want to drive out of his way or because he didn't have time, but because he was afraid of how the situation might be perceived, then or later. He explained that one of his personal rules was that he didn't give students rides—male or female. He didn't want to be perceived as having favorites or having it suggested that there was an improper relationship.

He explained that, for the same reason, he had removed the blinds that were on his interior office windows. He never used them anyway, but he didn't want to give anyone any reason to think he had anything to hide, he told the student.

These were his personal rules of behavior that he had established for himself as a way to try to remove any doubt about his ethics or his actions. No one had told him he couldn't give students rides home or that he needed to take down the blinds, but he had set his own standards.

That's what a leader does instinctively—they set higher standards of behavior for themselves.

I have my own rules of behavior that I follow at parties—you may have some, too. For example, I always leave early, before things can get crazy or out of hand (not that they ever do). But I want to be able to honestly claim that I had no knowledge of anything unprofessional that happened late in the evening. "I wasn't there," I can say, and no one will be able to refute me.

When I host get-togethers that include alcohol, I have a conversation with the bartender before the event and tell him or her that when I ask for a "glass," I'd like it to be mostly ginger ale with just a splash of Chardonnay for appearances. That way, I can appear to be drinking along with everyone else while still staying completely sober and lucid.

Leaders think about these scenarios in advance and plan how they'll handle them. They also share their thinking and their standards with others, to set expectations and model desired behavior.

You won't be mailing letters to the moon, so what are the most common unethical issues in business? Misuse of company time and resources is number one. This was the issue with Apollo 15. In business, the most common problems are use of company time and computers for personal use. Fraud is next. There are many different types of fraud, from employee theft to consumers returning of stolen goods. Plain old fairness is a universal issue. The perception of whether people are treated with equality and reciprocity is just that—perception. As managers we need to be able to explain the reasons and reasoning behind our actions.

Abusive behavior is the fastest growing issue and is receiving an increasing amount of press. The problem is abusive behavior among employees—particularly managers. Abusive behavior includes harassment, intimidation, profanity, and of course, physical touch.

You need to be careful that your own behavior isn't misinterpreted and that you're clear on standards for others.

Leadership Insight

Business ethics came into its own as a management field in the late 1960s. The newest branch of international business ethics did not emerge until the globalization of commerce around the turn of the century. There are no set of universal values. This differs by region, country, and often ethnic and religious groups. Leaders need to be aware of these differences. A general awareness of cultural dimensions is needed. In addition, I recommend that international managers be aware of the differing ethical traditions in different countries and the work of Transparency International and the annual survey of Corruption Perceptions Index (CPI).[72]

Setting standards can also help bring about desired change.

It has been said that Disney entertainment parks are so clean because Walt Disney paid attention to the little things and set the expectation that others should too. He made sure employees stayed on top of cleaning up any litter that hit the ground; they'd pick it up immediately. That led to pristine sidewalks and streets. And with clean surfaces, guests didn't want to be the one to dirty them—they look for garbage cans when they have trash, rather than just tossing them aside. The leader sets the norms of behavior for themselves, their teams, and for the organization.

Leadership Experience

Leaders need to be ready to set standards and show employees where the line is between ethical and unethical behavior. Sometimes, asking questions about various workplace scenarios can help you find that line and define it for others.

What are some ethical issues that could come up at work and how would you handle it? Thinking through a response in advance makes it quicker and easier to deal with infractions when they occur. Consider these questions:

- The money-making opportunities of postal covers is unique to a few occupations. What are the unique ethical risks in your business?

- Do you "model the way" with ethical behavior or do you cut corners to get things done?

- What have you done to inculcate humility as a value in yourself, your team, and your organization?

Different organizations have different standards, different lines they've drawn for employees to understand what behavior is expected. Your company may have written guidelines on some of these topics. Whether they do or don't, you should consider discussing these kinds of subjects with your team, so they know where you stand.

CHAPTER 12

APOLLO SOYUZ — CHANGING STRATEGIC INTENT

"The essence of strategy is choosing
what not to do."

—Michael Porter

The Apollo years were focused solely on getting to the moon to fulfill President John F. Kennedy's vision. That vision galvanized the nation because it focused the military, academia, the industrial sectors, and the scientific establishment all in the same direction. Internationally, it provided a peaceful way for east and west to compete for prominence. There was a lot riding on the space program. And the trifecta of them—Mercury, Gemini, and Apollo programs—were the winning combination in all areas. The economy, the Cold War, technology development, and the culture of the time were all shaped by the American drive to land on the moon. There was consensus around reaching the moon that unified the nation in a way that it could never be unified today.

In 1969, the Apollo 11 mission successfully met President John F. Kennedy's challenge to land a man on the moon and return him safely to Earth within the decade. The five successful moon landings cemented the victory, like a team running up the score after they beat an opponent. Even the "successful failure" of Apollo 13 was chalked up as a victory. But the race was over. Those final successes raised the question: what, if anything, was next for NASA?

The Encore Problem

Having reached the moon and achieved Kennedy's objective, there was a collective letdown—the typical ebb that occurs when any major goal is reached. In books and movies, this period following the story's climax is referred to as the falling action. In the case of Apollo, that downturn led to declining interest in space. The political will shifted. Funding ended for moon exploration. In organizational theory, this is an inflection point. It's the point at which an organization has succeeded, but the future is unclear and there appears to be two fundamental choices: obsolescence or reinvention.[73]

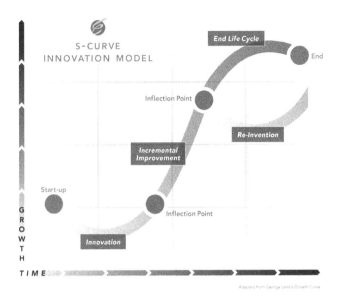

NASA is a federal government agency reporting to the president. On March 7, 1970, President Richard Nixon revealed his "Space Doctrine." This was the way NASA was to reinvent itself. Nixon believed NASA needed to transform itself from the do-or-die moon-landing space race to a more disciplined institution. Nixon said, "We must think of [space activities] as part of a continuing process... and not as a series of separate leaps, each requiring a massive concentration of energy. Space expenditures must take their proper place within a rigorous system of national priorities. ... What we do in space from here on in must become a normal and regular part of our national life and must therefore be planned in conjunction with all of the other undertakings which are important to us."

He went on to identify three tenets of his Space Doctrine.

1. NASA and the space program should be treated as one area of domestic policy competing with other concerns.

2. That the United States should limit its manned space flights to low-Earth orbit and to not begin a huge effort beyond that.

3. NASA's post-Apollo program should be constructed around a reusable space shuttle that could support yet-to-be-determined new objectives.

Nixon's Space Doctrine would have a longer lasting effect on the NASA organization than Kennedy's moon shot. Under Nixon, and then other presidents, NASA became just another domestic program, and the agency's budget decreased as it tried to find its new way.

The Rest of the Story

When President Nixon announced his Space Doctrine, one of the first places that felt the effect was rocket development, under Wernher von Braun. The Apollo 18, 19, and 20 were cancelled in 1970, but parts of the rockets for those missions had already been built. They ended up as displays in museums at three NASA centers (Johnson Space Center in Texas, Kennedy Space Center in Florida, and the Marshall Space Flight Center in Alabama) to recall the accomplishments of the Apollo program and to inspire the next generation of explorers.

A 1979 photo of the Saturn V rocket display at Johnson Space Center. The rocket has since been fully restored and a building added to protect it from the Texas weather.
NASA photo S79-40510

There is both an organizational and a personal side of the encore problem. For people, the question of what to do for a sequel or encore occurs fairly often. It's an issue for actors following their big break or after winning an Oscar. It's an issue for professionals who finally reach what they perceive to be the pinnacle

202 of their career in their field or in management

of their career in their field or in management. And organizationally it's an issue for companies that roll out a new product to major fanfare and demand, the life cycle end to a product, or when the market or competition end the success of years past. How can you reinvent yourself or your organization to an even bigger success or sometimes just survive?

This is a question that William Bridges studied with respect to change. His "Transition Model,"[74] which he covered in depth in his book, *Managing Transitions*, distinguished between change, which happens to us, and transition, which is the internal process of how we deal and cope with the change that is thrust upon us. Change can happen instantly, such as with the loss of a job or the cancellation of a program, but processing and accepting that change can take much longer.

According to Bridges, there are three stages of change: 1) Ending, losing, and letting go; 2) The neutral zone; 3) The new beginning.

- **Ending, losing, and letting go.** This stage, when people are often in a state of shock, is generally filled with fear, anger, and resentment, much like the initial stages of grief. There may also be denial and fear, along with some disorientation as people try and get their bearings. They're often sad and nervous about how their lives will be impacted. Communication and empathy are crucial at this point. Unless you acknowledge and address these emotions, Bridges says, it will be nearly impossible for people to let go of the old and move on to the new.

- **The neutral zone.** In stage two, as people process what is happening, they often feel anxiety, low morale, and skepticism about the future, or whether it will be better than the past. You will often see a decline in productivity and morale, as employees either adjust to new processes and ways of doing things or work through their nervousness about what's to come. For the organization this is often a time of resource disruption. What people, process, and equipment are surplus and what is still needed? It can also be a time of renewed innovation. Often the organizational barriers and protocols break down. For employees it can be a period of creativity as they discover their freedom to try new things.

- **The new beginning.** In the last stage, as people begin to accept and even embrace the new changes, you'll see more energy and excitement start to emerge. Many people look for new opportunities to learn and are curious about what this will mean for them. There is often a renewed commitment to the organization as people start to see what's possible in the future. They begin to look ahead, not back.

At NASA, the organization's success at managing these stages varied. The agency did find ways to continue a less ambitious human exploration program. But, deep space robotic missions, such as the Voyager spacecraft, received increased funding. Under engineering legends like Max Faget, the agency designed and developed the "Space Transportation System" to ferry humans into low-Earth orbit. The organization aimed to remain flexible and at-the-ready should a new initiative require its sudden focus. It accomplished this adaptability and flexibility by keeping the government population on its payroll small. That is, its employee count was deliberately kept low. Instead, it relies on contractors from universities and outside suppliers to fill in its human resources as needed. But it was still a case of do more with less.

The people felt this struggle. There are people who are still bitter over the change from NASA's special mission to being just another domestic agency.

Celebrating the End

Savvy leaders take the opportunity to help their employees grapple with change that has been forced on them, sometimes suddenly and typically through no fault of their own.

It's human nature to mark the beginning and end of important times in our lives. We have celebrations on the birth of a child, at baptisms, confirmations, Bar and Bat Mitzvahs, graduations, retirement, marriages, and, in some cases, divorces. We mark the occasion by holding a special event. That event signals the end of the period of life that happened before and the start of something new.

In the case of NASA, employees had to process the fact that their mission was no longer to get a man on the moon—they had done that. But there was no party, no big meeting to congratulate the key participants. It was just over. Done. As a result, many people had trouble moving on.

That tendency to want to hold onto the past is natural. But, in business it can be disruptive or a road-block to progress. This fact is likely why one of my former colleagues at IBM used to make a huge deal when organizational shifts occurred.

I was invited to witness one, which occurred at the Rye Brook Hilton in Westchester, New York. It just so happened that I was staying at the Hilton for an IBM project and bumped into a friend of mine who worked in IBM's office products (OP) division. He said, "Want to see something cool? Come with me," and then led me down to the hotel bar.

I was surprised to see so many IBM employees gathered there—I was unsure for what—and then a manager stepped up and spoke to the group. "We are in a time of transitions," he told them. "Follow me outside."

The group followed him out to the front lawn of the Hilton hotel where there was an area that had been cordoned off and a big hole that had been dug.

"It has been announced that OP won't exist next week," he told everyone. "So, let's take the opportunity to think about all of our accomplishments while we were part of this division." And he began holding up products, artifacts, really, that had been conceived and developed within the group. Products like the famous Selectric ball, magnetic media, or MagCard typewriters, and ink jet printers.

"We're going to bury our past, which is OP," he told us, and then proceeded to put the box of products into the hole in the ground. Then members of the team took turns taking a shovel of dirt and scooping it onto the box, much like funeral attendees do into a grave.

"Now let's celebrate all that we accomplished. Monday we'll be part of data processing," he said, as he invited everyone back in to the bar to share stories about their days in OP, much like what happens at an Irish wake. And the employees did. They remembered, they told stories, they laughed as they reminisced, and they grieved the ending of their careers in OP together, reassuring each other that everything would be okay.

This leader understood the importance of marking the end of an era and to celebrate the many wins the group had enjoyed, so that they could begin a new era in their careers the following week. The ceremonial burial of OP artifacts marked the official end of that division, helping employees to understand that its closure was truly the end.

Their time together at the bar helped them get from that sense of loss, in Bridges' stage one, to the neutral zone, where they could begin to process and accept that something new was coming, and by the end of the evening, they were feeling better about what Monday morning held for them and could look ahead with anticipation, rather than dread, toward their new beginning.

Leadership Insight

Many companies are realizing the power of storytelling to create and preserve their organization's culture. But we often overlook the power of artifacts and rituals. NASA is very consciously using both to symbolize their past and future. Look at this photograph of Mission Control. Notice the plaques on the wall. All of the successful missions that were flown from that room are up there. At the conclusion of each mission, the flight directors select a person, or sometimes a team, that best exemplified the values of the organization during the mission. There is a ceremony attended by the astronauts, flight teams, and executives to honor the selected person. That individual signs the back of the plaque and climbs a ladder to hang the plaque. It is never taken down.

Now notice the four plaques by the door, with the light shining on them. Those are the plaques of NASA's greatest failures: Challenger, Columbia, and Apollo 1, where astronauts died. The fourth plaque is the Flight Operations Directorate emblem representing the organization's duty to keep astronauts safe. These plaques are next to the door to remind everyone as they pass that people's lives depend on the work done in this room.

The use of artifacts in Mission Control is not unusual at NASA. Every department and every building have artifacts and mementos that speak to the unique culture of that place.

The Environment Changed

These times are a changing. In the US, President Nixon had the task of helping the American public move on from the end of the race to the moon to what was next, whatever that was. He acknowledged, "We've accomplished the dream," following the sixth moon landing, letting Americans know that the space race was over. As a major reinvention, Nixon envisioned a 180-degree move, from competition in space to collaboration. One of Nixon's first initiatives was the Apollo-Soyuz Test Project, which started as a peace mission.

The Rest of the Story

The Apollo-Soyuz mission wasn't a magic bullet that ended years of competition and distrust between the Soviet Union and the United States. For the Americans, there were months of Russian language training and flying between the two countries to become familiar with the Soyuz system. The Soviets also learned English and visited NASA. On the surface it appeared very collegial, but the lack of trust was still there.

The rooms given to the Americans in the Soviet Union were bugged. But the Americans figured out a way to use that to their advantage. Said Deke Slayton: "One day we decided to test it, and complained loudly that we didn't have anything to do. 'Too bad we don't have a pool table.' The next day, by God, there was a pool table in our bar downstairs," he wrote in his autobiography, *Deke!*[75]

The competitive spirit was still alive on both sides. While Americans refer to the program as "Apollo-Soyuz," Russians referred to it as "Soyuz-Apollo," reflecting the national pride each felt for their role.

On July 17, 1975, an American Apollo spacecraft docked with a Russian Soyuz space capsule in space, connecting the countries' technology and astronauts.

While in space, the three American astronauts and two cosmonauts did press conferences together and had photos taken of them shaking hands and eating together, reinforcing the sense that this was a new beginning of US-Russian relations. The nations had moved from competing with each other to collaborating. They worked together on several experiments for two days before disconnecting, "deorbiting," and returning to their respective homes.

An article on Space.com states this about the Apollo-Soyuz Test Project (ASTP):[76]

"ASTP was a signal that the Space Race was over. The two nations, now fighting different foes other than themselves and facing budgetary restrictions for spaceflight, openly spoke of working together in future initiatives."

It was evidence of a redirection of strategic intent. That historic mission was the first step to a series of collaborative space projects that culminated in the development of the International Space Station.

The Rest of the Story

Would you like to see the results of NASA's change of strategic intent from your own backyard?

You can easily see the International Space Station (ISS) with the naked eye if you know when and where to look. Go to https://spotthestation.nasa.gov. There you can sign up for text or email notifications that will give you the exact time and location in the sky so that you can see the ISS pass. When you view it, think of the six international astronauts riding inside at 17,500 miles per hour and all of the leadership and management expertise it took to get them there.

With the US and Russia working together, the countries created a new vision of the future. Working through initial distrust and patriotic pride about their own technology, the astronauts and cosmonauts found common ground in continuing space exploration. They agreed to work together to build a space station that would be accessible to many countries. Both sides agreed on this new direction, this new beginning that ultimately involved twenty-nine other countries.

Leadership Insight

Henry Kissinger told George Low, "You can do anything else you want as long as you achieve peaceful cooperation with the Russians." This is a good example of two leadership principles. First, it makes clear the leader's strategic intent—peaceful cooperation. Second, it defines the degree of autonomy for the subordinate. In this case it was any action that didn't interfere with the strategic intent. This is often described as "freedom within a framework." Leaders do this so that people know what they can and can't do. A manager might say you can change the process as long as you stay within budget and on schedule. Freedom to change, but the framework is money and time.

Signaling Change by "North Winding"

The winds of change. Another approach you can use in leading change is called north winding. I had never heard the term "north winding," other than with respect to the cold front announced on the weather report.

Turns out, the phrase refers both to the bitter weather that moves through during winter and the communication technique that warns of coming change.

When you look at a weather forecast indicating a cold front is coming, you'll see a low-pressure area right in front of it, drawing the cold air in. Right before that low-pressure area, however, is a north wind. The north wind announces the coming change in temperature, warning of discomfort not far behind.

The term "north winding" refers to a similar warning used in communication. It is a proactive technique used by managers to soften the blow of coming information or change. For example, if a senior manager knows that job cuts are coming in the next few weeks, he or she might start to share information about the company missing its financial targets, suggesting poor sales, or report that another department just had to cut five percent of its staff. That manager might not have authorization to leak details of the coming cuts, but he or she can certainly begin to softly introduce the idea that their team might ultimately be impacted.

Then when the news is announced, employees aren't totally shocked and taken off-guard—after all, they'd been hearing whispers for a while that cuts might occur.

I try to do this within my own company. For example, while sales have been well above our goal for a couple of years, if we wanted to scale back on expenses as a buffer against a downturn, I might tell my team that, "I think we may have to reduce travel next year."

I haven't said that sales are down or that we're going to have to tighten our belts, but that to shore up our reserves, we might want to rely more on technology to meeting with out-of-town prospects.

That's north winding—giving employees a heads up that change may be headed our way. It doesn't involve sounding an alarm or creating drama where there isn't any, but introducing the notion that just because things have been going one way for months doesn't mean they will continue to go the same way forever.

North winding is another technique you can use to soften the blow of impending change, to help employees move from the first stage of ending, losing, and letting go, as Bridges identifies it, and on to the neutral zone in preparation for a new beginning.

You can use this technique to help your team understand when changes in strategic intent may be coming.

Leadership Experience

The higher you climb within an organization, the sooner you know about impending changes before they occur. To employees on the front line, announcements about layoffs, reorganizations, or other changes can seem out of nowhere—they may feel shocked. But leaders at the top, who have been part of the decision-making process and the weighing of options, may feel like it's old news once the big announcement is made.

To help prepare your team for change that you expect may be or know is coming, without sharing the news prematurely, actively explore the following:

- How much do your people know about the current business? How can I keep them informed?

- What are the rumors that are circulating out there?

- What do they need to know? To help them prepare, consider north winding them.

- What are they feeling? Are they scared or excited?

- What do you want them to do? Is there anything they can do in preparation?

A mentor of mine told me that in order to influence people, you need to have answers in your own mind to three questions:

1. What do I want people to know?

2. What do I want people to feel?

3. What do I want people to do?

Approaches such as north winding are simply ways to address those three questions. The more you can make employees aware of possible changes in the organization, the better prepared they will be emotionally, mentally, and even financially. Helping them move from that sense of loss into a neutral zone early will give them a competitive advantage they will greatly appreciate.

EPILOGUE

Many of the leadership insights that came out of NASA are still there, sixty years later. The people who grappled with tough situations, made difficult decisions, and led challenging teams left a lasting legacy from which we all continue to benefit.

Walk into Building 30 at the Johnson Space Center and on the corner of many of the whiteboards—there are no longer chalkboards on the walls—you'll see the words "Tough" and "Competent" handwritten and blocked off so that they won't be erased. Those are Gene Kranz's hallowed terms for NASA engineers that he, long ago, dictated should be etched on the board. They serve as a constant reminder of how determined and resilient the organization's employees are. They were then and they are now, tough and competent.

Or stop by the Biergarten at Marshall Space Flight Center on a Thursday night for beer and brats and you'll get a sense of what it was like decades ago, when German scientists gathered after working on rockets all day. Wernher von Braun started that tradition. Although he worked hard to become more American, he also wanted to honor his heritage. The Biergarten was his attempt to remain connected to his past. For NASA engineers, it became the local watering hole.

When I conduct workshops at Johnson Space Center, we visit the Astronaut Memorial Grove where an oak tree has been planted for every deceased astronaut. At that sober spot I ask people to recall a time when a leader said or did something that deeply affected them. Some people have trouble thinking of an example. I've never had a NASA person hesitate to cite a time when a NASA leader had an impact on their lives.

By the same token, the legend of great leaders lives on as well. Leaders like Wernher von Braun, George Low, and Glynn Lunney made their mark on the Apollo program that can still be felt today.

Research has shown that seventy percent of what we learn about work we pick up at work. Twenty percent we learn from other sources, such as reading articles and blog posts or TV and radio. And ten percent we learn through leadership training.

That means that a good portion of what NASA employees today learn was likely influenced or shaped by Apollo leaders decades ago. All of those managers left lessons that we continue to learn from today.

So, as you consider what kind of leader you aspire to be, also think about what legacy you want to leave behind. What contribution do you want to make? How can you change your organization for the better? What do you want to be remembered for? Then what do you need to do to make that a reality?

ACKNOWLEDGEMENTS

There are so many people to acknowledge for their help with this book. Alex D'Eath encouraged me to write and told me when I was wrong. Glynn Lunney made sure I gave credit where credit was due. The many people at NASA's history division answered my questions with patience and accuracy. Most of the photos are from NASA's Image and Video Library. Fellow space collector David Frohman let me use his photo of Buzz Aldrin's chalice.

Alex and Glynn reviewed chapters as did Harv Hartman, Peter Orton, Margaret Richardson, Doug Ward, John Wattendorf, and Morgan Yeagan. I drew upon the leadership and management knowledge of numerous people I've known over the years. As I reread chapters I recognize many people's influence including old IBM colleagues Jerry Cushing, Ron Dibble, Susan Gerke, Nancy Lewis, and John Wattendorf. I've learned a great deal from NASA leaders including Arnie Aldridge, Brian Duffy, Matt Gray, Norm Knight, Dave Leestma, Ellen Ochoa, and Holly Ridings. Harv Hartman is a special friend who has opened doors at NASA for me and opened my mind to new ideas.

Thank you to my workmate Marcia Layton Turner and my coach and teacher Peter Orton. Stephanie Chandler guided me through the publishing process.

ENDNOTES

1. Price, Edward, "Rocket," Britannica.com. https://www.britannica.com/technology/rocket-jet-propulsion-device-and-vehicle

2. "Wernher von Braun," WernhervonBraunrocket blog, http://wernhervonbraunrocket.blogspot.com/p/blog-page_6179.html

3. Walker, Andrew, "Project Paperclip: Dark Side of the Moon," BBC News, 11/21/05 http://news.bbc.co.uk/2/hi/uk_news/magazine/4443934.stm

4. Ibid

5. Wright, Mike-Marshall Space Flight Historian, "The Disney-Von Braun Collaboration and its Influence on Space Exploration," Marshall Space Flight Center History Office, 1993 https://history.msfc.nasa.gov/vonbraun/disney_article.html

6. Heifetz, Ronald and Martin Linsky, "A Survival Guide for Leaders," *Harvard Business Review*, June 2002 https://hbr.org/2002/06/a-survival-guide-for-leaders

7. "The First 100 Days: John F. Kenney," Presidential History Geeks, 5/2/17 https://potus-geeks.livejournal.com/842865.html

8. Wall, Mike, "JFK's Moon Shot: Q&A with Space Policy Expert John Logsdon," Space.com, 5/24/11 https://www.space.com/11762-nasa-kennedy-moon-speech-logsdon-interview.html

9. "I'm not that interested in space," NASA history blog https://history.nasa.gov/JFK-Webbconv/pages/backgnd.html#interest

10. "John F. Kennedy Moon Speech – Rice Stadium," 9/12/62

11. "Lincoln at Gettysburg," Abraham Lincoln online http://www.abrahamlincolnonline.org/lincoln/sites/gettysburg.htm

12. Quote Investigator, 3/1/14 https://quoteinvestigator.com/2014/03/01/short-speech/

13. Gallo, Carmine, "The Science Behind TED's 18-Minute Rule," LinkedIn Pulse, 3/13/14 https://www.linkedin.com/pulse/20140313205730-5711504-the-science-behind-ted-s-18-minute-rule/

14. Ibid

15. Bizony, Piers, *The Man Who Ran The Moon; James E. Webb, NASA, and the Secret History of Project Apollo*, NY: Thunder's Mouth Press, 2006, p. 8

16. Ibid

17. Ibid

18. Logsdon, John, *John F. Kennedy and the Race to the Moon*, Palgrave Macmillan; NY, 2013, p. 42

19. Ibid

20. Dunning, David, "We Are All Confident Idiots," Pacific Standard, 10/27/14 https://psmag.com/social-justice/confident-idiots-92793

21. Weiss, Antonio, *101 Business Ideas that Will Change the Way You Work: Turning Clever Thinking into Smart Advice*, Pearson Education; UK, 2013, p. 29

22. "Michael Jordan Chronology," Tar Heels website, 4/17/03 https://goheels.com/news/2003/4/17/205473895.aspx

23. Willett, Brian, "Michael Jordan's Baseball History, Livestrong website https://www.livestrong.com/article/36 5378-michael-jordans-baseball-history/

24. Seamans, Robert C., Jr. et al, *Project Apollo: The Touch Decisions* (Seamans Report), Washington, DC: NASA, 2005, p. 16

25. Chan, Chris, "Phil Jackson: A Coach For All Players," *Bleacher Report*, 6/15/09 https://bleacherreport.com/articles/199808-phil-jackson-best-coach-ever

26. Daniels, Dave, "Phil Jackson Made Disciplinary Allowances for Dennis Rodman," Pippen Ain't Easy, 9/10/25 https://pippenainteasy.com/2015/09/10/phil-jackson-made-disciplinary-allowances-for-dennis-rodman/

27. Kraft, Chris, *FLIGHT: My Life in Mission Control*, Dutton, New York; 2001, p. 68

28. Ibid, p. 2

29. "Near-Mutiny on Apollo 7: Colds, Tempers Marred Mission," Seeker.com, 10/23/13 https://www.seeker.

com/near-mutiny-on-apollo-7-colds-tempers-marred-mission-1767965064.html

30. "Retrospective: A Speech by Wernher von Braun on Management," 1962, Medium.com https://medium.com/@telluric/dr-wernher-von-braun-director-96eeae675528

31. Brown, Tim, *Changes by Design: How Design Thinking Transforms Organizations and Inspires Innovation*, HarperBusiness; NY, 2009

32. Hansen, Morten, "IDEO CEO Tim Brown: T-Shapred Stars: The Backbone of IDEO's Collaborative Culture, *Chief Executive*, 1/21/10 https://chiefexecutive.net/ideo-ceo-tim-brown-t-shaped-stars-the-backbone-of-ideoaes-collaborative-culture__trashed/

33. Careers in Medicine, American Association of Medical Colleges list https://www.aamc.org/cim/specialty/exploreoptions/list/

34. Retrospective: A Speech by Wernher von Braun on Management," 1962, Medium.com https://medium.com/@telluric/dr-wernher-von-braun-director-96eeae675528

35. More, Chris, "I am T-shaped. Are you too? Learn from my story," Medium.com, 2/12/18 https://medium.com/@chrismore/i-am-t-shaped-an-origin-story-a91bf5a546c6

36. Retrospective: A Speech by Wernher von Braun on Management," 1962, Medium.com https://medium.com/@telluric/dr-wernher-von-braun-director-96eeae675528

37. Bartlett, Christopher and Sumantra Ghoshal, "What is a Global Manager?" *Harvard Business Review*, August 2003 https://hbr.org/2003/08/what-is-a-global-manager

38. Retrospective: A Speech by Wernher von Braun on Management," 1962, Medium.com https://medium.com/@telluric/dr-wernher-von-braun-director-96eeae675528

39. Colby, Tanner, *Some of My Best Friends Are Black: The Strange Story of Integration in America*, Penguin Books; NY, 2013, p. 205

40. "Katherine Johnson Interview: NASA's Human Computer," History vs Hollywood http://www.historyvshollywood.com/video/katherine-johnson-interview-nasa/

41. "'Hidden Figures': How Black Women Did the Math that Put Men on the Moon," All Things Considered, NPR, 9/25/16 https://www.npr.org/2016/09/25/495179824/hidden-figures-how-black-women-did-the-math-that-put-men-on-the-moon

42. Lunney, Glynn, *Highways Into Space*, self-published, 2014, p34

43. "Apollo XIII Flight Director Glynn Lunney Talks About Leadership," Friendswood Library talk, 11/20/15 https://www.youtube.com/watch?v=phMnI37y1lI

44. Ibid

45. Strack, Rainer, "Decoding Global Talent," Boston Consulting Group, 10/6/14 https://www.bcg.com/publications/2014/people-organization-human-resources-decoding-global-talent.aspx

46. Ibid

47. Best Places to Work in the Federal Government https://bestplacestowork.org

48. Mann, Annamarie, "Why We Need Best Friends at Work," Gallup, 1/15/18 https://www.gallup.com/workplace/236213/why-need-best-friends-work.aspx

49. "State of the American Manager," Gallup, https://www.gallup.com/services/182138/state-american-manager.aspx?utm_source=gbj&utm_medium=copy&utm_campaign=20150421-gbj

50. Beck, Randall and Jim Harter, "Managers Account for 70% of Variance in Employee Engagement," Gallup, 4/21/15 https://news.gallup.com/businessjournal/182792/managers-account-variance-employee-engagement.aspx

51. Ou, Amy et al, "Do Humble CEOs Matter" An Examination of CEO Humility and Firm Outcomes," *Journal of Management*, 9/21/15 https://journals.sagepub.com/doi/abs/10.1177/0149206315604187

52. MacCormack, Alan, "Management Lessons from Mars," *Harvard Business Review*, May 2004 https://hbr.org/2004/05/management-lessons-from-mars

53. "Peanuts Marks 50 Years in Space with New NASA Mission for Snoopy," CollectSpace.com, 7/10/18 http://www.collectspace.com/news/news-071018a-nasa-peanuts-snoopy-space-act.html

54. Hogan Assessments https://www.hoganassessments.com

55. Richardson, Dick, "Lessons from Sully, part 3: Self-Awareness and Rituals," ExperiencetoLead.com https://www.experiencetolead.com/sully-self-awareness/

56. Hoque, Faisal, "10 Ways to Stay Calm in the Face of Daily Stress," *Fast Company*, 2/10/15 https://www.fastcompany.com/3042153/10-steps-to-keep-calm-and-carry-on

57. De Bono, Edward, "Six Thinking Hats," http://www.debonothinkingsystems.com/tools/6hats.htm

58. Jurek, Richard, "The Man Who Won the Moon Race," *Air & Space Magazine*, December 2018 https://www.airspacemag.com/space/apollo-8-george-low-profile-180970807/#q8XO626YBrMLgFBL.99

59. Goleman, Daniel, "Brain's Design Emerges as a Key to Emotions," *New York Times*, 8/15/89 https://www.

nytimes.com/1989/08/15/science/brain-s-design-emerges-as-a-key-to-emotions.html?pagewanted=all

60. Västfjäll, D., and P. Slovic, "Cognition and emotion in judgment and decision making," In M. D. Robinson, E. R. Watkins, & E. Harmon-Jones (Eds.), *Handbook of cognition and emotion* (pp. 252–271). Guilford Press; NY, 2013, p 252-271

61. "A Bold Course of Action," PBS.org https://www.pbs.org/wgbh/americanexperience/features/moon-apollo-8s-firsts/

62. "Reporting on the INS," Winter 2002 https://niemanreports.org/issues/winter-2002/

63. "There's a Critical Difference Between Creativity and Innovation," Business Insider, 4/10/13 https://www.businessinsider.com/difference-between-creativity-and-innovation-2013-4

64. Levitt, Theodore, "Creativity is Not Enough," *Harvard Business Review*, August 2002 https://hbr.org/2002/08/creativity-is-not-enough

65. Ranadive, Ameet, "The Rule of 3," Medium, 5/28/13 https://medium.com/lessons-from-mckinsey/the-rule-of-3-c1cd82dbc96e

66. Gallo, Carmine, "Thomas Jefferson, Steve Jobs, and the Rule of 3," *Forbes*, 7/2/12 https://www.forbes.com/sites/carminegallo/2012/07/02/thomas-jefferson-steve-jobs-and-the-rule-of-3/#69f8726c1962

67. https://www.jsc.nasa.gov/history/oral_histories/HaiseFW/HaiseFW_3-23-99.htm

68. Slayton, Deke, *Deke! US Manned Space: From Mercury to the Shuttle*, Forge; NY, 1995, p. 278-279, 5171-5180

69. Owen, David and Jonathan Davidson, "Hubris Syndrome: An acquired personality disorder? A study of US

Presidents and UK Prime Ministers over the last 100 years," *Brain*, Vol. 132, Issue, 5, May 2009, p. 1396-1406 https://academic.oup.com/brain/article/132/5/1396/354862

70. Pedicini, Sandra, "Worker fired, rehired over tweet about gators at Disney World," Orlando Sentinel, 7/15/16 https://www.orlandosentinel.com/business/tourism/os-disney-gator-employee-twitter-fired-20160715-story.html

71. Ferris, Stephen et al, "CEO Overconfidence and International Merger and Acquisition Activity," *Journal of Financial and Quantitative Analysis*, Vol. 48, Issue 1, February 2013 https://doi.org/10.1017/S0022109013000069

72. Transparency International https://www.transparency.org

73. Land, George and Beth Jarman, *Breakpoint and Beyond: Mastering the Future Today*, Leadership 2000 Inc., 8/1/98 https://www.amazon.com/Breakpoint-Beyond-Mastering-Future-Today/dp/0962660523

74. "Bridges' Transition Model," MindTools https://www.mindtools.com/pages/article/bridges-transition-model.htm

75. Slayton, Deke, *Deke! US Manned Space: From Mercury to the Shuttle*, Forge; NY, 1995, p. 278-279, 5171-5180

76. Howell, Elizabeth, "Apollo-Soyuz Test Project: Americans, Russians Meet in Space," Space.com, 4/25/13 https://www.space.com/20833-apollo-soyuz.html

ABOUT THE AUTHOR

Dick Richardson is an executive leadership development consultant. He is the owner of Experience to Lead, offering unique experiences to improve the leadership of individuals, teams, and organizations. His firm offers a variety of immersive programs for senior leaders including the Apollo Leadership Experience. His relationships with NASA, the Smithsonian Institution, Space Center Houston, and Kennedy Space Center have allowed unique behind-the-scenes access for executives to learn the inner workings of the nation's space program. *Apollo Leadership Lessons* is a result of his work with NASA executives and astronauts.

Prior to working as an independent consultant, Dick was director of executive leadership development for ITT. Before that, he held a variety of leadership positions in executive and management development at IBM. He holds two patents for innovations in organizational learning. Dick's international experience includes being responsible for IBM management development for IBM Asia, based in Hong Kong, and numerous other overseas assignments. He has been recognized with numerous industry awards in leadership development and learning.

Learn more: ExperiencetoLead.com.

CPSIA information can be obtained
at www.ICGtesting.com
Printed in the USA
LVHW052348170419
614553LV00003B/5/P